D0356351

TWO WEEKS IN
COSTA RICA

TWO WEEKS IN COSTA RICA

MATTHEW HOUDE

JENNIFER TURNBULL

TRAVELOGUE ADVENTURES

Copyright © 2012 by Matthew Houde and Jennifer Turnbull

Photographs and map copyright © 2012 by Matthew Houde and Jennifer Turnbull

All rights reserved. No part of this book may be reproduced or transmitted in any form or by any means, electronic or mechanical, including photocopying, recording, or by any information storage and retrieval system, without written permission from the publisher, except by a reviewer who may quote brief passages in a review.

Published by Travelogue Adventures, Cambridge, Massachusetts.
www.twoweeksincostarica.com

Printed in the United States of America

ISBN: 978-0-9850769-3-1

DISCLAIMER

This book describes the authors' experiences while traveling in Costa Rica and reflects their opinions related to those experiences. Conversations are written as accurately as can be remembered and are not intended to be exact quotations. Some names and identifying details of individuals mentioned have been changed to protect their privacy.

This book is intended to provide helpful and informative material on the subjects addressed herein. Although the information provided was accurate as of publication, things can change quickly in Costa Rica so it's best to check schedules, prices, and rates before traveling to obtain the most current information. The authors have taken all reasonable care in preparing this book, but they make no warranty about its accuracy or completeness and, to the maximum extent permitted, disclaim all liability arising from its use.

CONTENTS

Contents

LIST OF SIDEBARS

List of Sidebars

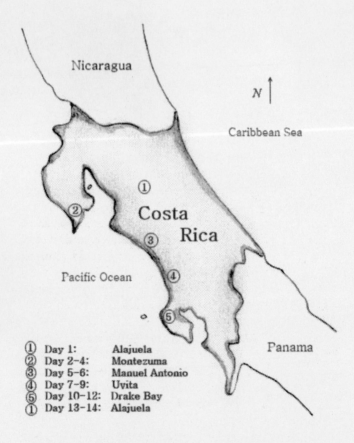

Nicaragua

N

Caribbean Sea

Costa Rica

Pacific Ocean

Panama

① Day 1:   Alajuela
② Day 2-4:   Montezuma
③ Day 5-6:   Manuel Antonio
④ Day 7-9:   Uvita
⑤ Day 10-12: Drake Bay
① Day 13-14: Alajuela

INTRODUCTION

Six years ago, my wife, Jenn, and I knew nothing about Costa Rica. To us it was just a mysterious tropical paradise somewhere in Central America. Then we met Roy, a temporary coworker of mine who grew up and lived there. During the two years he was in the States, we became close friends. Every time we got together, Roy would captivate us with another story about Costa Rica. Whether it was seeing an erupting volcano, watching baby sea turtles hatch, or encountering a sloth, we couldn't get enough of his tales of living in such an exotic place.

When Roy left to go back home, he gave us just one thing: a guidebook to Costa Rica. I think he knew that the book, along with the stories he had told, would persuade us to visit. He was right. Five trips later, we are still discovering why Roy was so proud to share Costa Rica with us.

Yes, it has beautiful beaches, nearly perfect weather, good food, and all the comforts of vacation, but it is Costa Rica's unparalleled ability to slow the pace of life that makes it so special. Each time we visit, Jenn and I arrive highly strung and stressed from work and our busy everyday lives. Costa Rica and its people seem to welcome us by showing how beautiful and simple life can be. At the same time, the wild natural environment awakens our sense of adventure and inspires us to get out of our comfort zones. This balance of relaxation and adventure is what leaves us coming back, year after year.

This book was written to share our fondness for Costa Rica. Much like Roy did for us, we tell a story about Costa Rica while providing information you'll need to travel there. We do this by weaving together two genres of travel writing, narrative and guidebook. We felt that writing only a narrative would leave many questions unanswered; similarly, writing only a guidebook would provide limited cultural and personal perspective. By reading this book, you'll get both: the personal story of one of our most memorable vacations and practical travel tips and information. You'll gain an understanding of Costa Rica's culture and learn how the country is best traveled. From exploring national parks to local lingo and navigating the airport, this book will give you the foundation to create your own great adventure in Costa Rica.

* * *

To read our blog, learn more about traveling in Costa Rica, and see more photos and videos, visit us at http://www.twoweeksincostarica.com.

Find us on Facebook at http://www.facebook.com/TwoWeeksInCostaRica.

Follow us on Twitter at @2wksinCR.

EVERY DAY

THE DAILY GRIND

I couldn't believe it, it was still snowing. I sat in my plow truck thinking about the last twenty-four hours. I had left my house in Boston around two o'clock in the afternoon the day before, just as the snowflakes were starting to fall. I got to the office and started my truck's stubborn diesel engine, knowing that I would be stuck in the cab for the next day or so. I packed my new home with everything one would need to plow for a twenty-four-hour snowstorm, mostly lots of coffee and unhealthy snacks. As I pulled out of the driveway, I shook my head, thinking that I had done this just three days ago.

Twenty hours and eighteen inches of snow later, it was now ten in the morning, although it still felt like the middle of the night. The floor of my truck was littered with junk-food wrappers, wet gloves, and empty coffee cups. I was slouched over the wheel in an old sweatshirt, my brown hair peeking out from a wool hat and plastered to my sweaty forehead. My eyes were bloodshot, my mind fatigued. The five commercial parking lots around Boston that I was charged with keeping clear of snow had kept me up all night. Just when I had cleaned one down to the pavement, I would arrive at the next to see that four inches more already had accumulated since my last pass; it was a vicious cycle.

I turned the radio to the weather. The meteorologist reported that the mighty nor'easter that had been circling Boston for the last day, dumping snow off the ocean, would finally retreat by three o'clock. I hoped he was right. If he was, I would probably make it home by seven or eight tonight, a thirty-hour shift.

* * *

Across town, in a red brick office building near Boston's financial district, the words on a computer screen blurred together into a fuzzy gray collage. Regulatory filings and documents with footnotes longer than the page itself, the dry writing of lawyers and economists, filled the screen. My wife, Jenn, a lawyer herself, sat in a desk chair, like she did every day, clicking through the complex nest of documents open on her desktop. Her six-by-six cubicle consisted of a desk, computer, filing cabinet, bookshelf, and lots of files. The dividing walls were short, ensuring absolutely no privacy, and the overhead lights cast an artificial glow over her long brown hair.

Jenn works for a state agency that regulates utility companies. Most people have no idea what she does and quickly lose interest when she tries to explain her job. Ratemaking surely is not a mainstream concept that too many people have heard of, but Jenn enjoys it. Today, though, even she had had enough. The last year at work had left her feeling burned out. Her usual nine to five had become eight to eight plus weekends. In fact, she was spending so much time at the office that she was even getting to know the nighttime cleaning crew. Unable to focus on what she was writing, she decided it was time for a coffee break.

Jenn enthusiastically clicked each window closed until she reached her computer background. A colorful picture popped up. It was the two of us on a beach in Costa Rica. We were sitting on a rock, the lush greenery of the rainforest bordering the sand; our smiles were big, our skin tanned. The picture was taken the winter before exactly one year to the day.

Jenn took a deep breath and closed her eyes, letting herself relax. When she opened them again, something on the edge of the screen caught her attention. It was a yellow Post-it note, which read, "Costa Rica trip: buy plane tickets, order new backpack, find swim shoes, get snorkels out of closet." Each item on the list had been struck through with a red pen. Jenn typed one final e-mail before logging off, then grabbed her bag and left.

* * *

In the back corner of a parking lot, my truck idled, its bright yellow plow cocked to one side and wipers swaying rhythmically. I watched with a blank stare as a few determined workers began to show up for the day, carefully navigating their vehicles across the slick lot with frosted windows and ledges of snow hanging off their roofs. My phone vibrated, an e-mail coming through. This was about the time of day that the second round of residential clients would start complaining about their driveways needing to be cleared, the first round being the early risers at about six o'clock. We had already dealt with them. Apparently my crews had been doing a good job since then because this message wasn't from a client, it was from Jenn.

> Hi, you're still out, right? Did you sleep at all? I'm sorry it's still snowing. Here is a picture that might cheer you up. We're leaving in exactly one week, you know!
> -Jenn

DAY 1

SMARTPHONE WITHDRAWAL AND A NOISY GAME OF BRIDGE

Groggy and tired, we opened our front door to the sound of the 5:45 bus rushing away. Left in a trail of slush, we ambled along the dark sidewalk toward the subway station on foot. Delicate snowflakes veiled our heads in white and added to the shoulder-high snow piles that barricaded the streets. A slick layer of ice made it difficult to walk, but we trekked on, eager to escape.

Sure, the weather was typical for February in Massachusetts, but it had been an exceptionally hard winter even by New England standards. Storm after storm had pummeled Boston with over eighty inches of snow, and with temperatures staying brutally cold, the piles just kept growing. Even the diehard Bostonians who always tout, "I love the snow; winter's my favorite season," were cursing their own words.

Having both grown up in Maine, Jenn and I were used to the cold and snow, but even we had had enough. We desperately needed some sun and adventure. So off we went, shivering, in our much too lightweight clothing, having opted to leave behind our wool coats and knitted hats for cotton shirts and jeans—the warmest clothes we would need for the next two weeks.

After a slow ten-minute walk on the slippery sidewalk, we finally made it to the subway station. At this early hour, the escalators, turnstiles, and benches were all but deserted. The rush-hour chaos that Jenn encountered on her daily commute would not be for another couple of hours. As we waited anxiously on the platform for an inbound train to downtown Boston, the layer of snow on our clothes melted away, making our skin feel dewy. Light soon appeared in the tunnel, and the train pulled into the station with a whir.

Lugging along our gigantic backpacks, we jumped off the subway and entered Logan International Airport. We passed through security, found the nearest cup of coffee, and started to wake up. Our gate was quiet with mostly business travelers reading e-mails or morning newspapers. A man sitting across from us, sharply dressed in a dark gray suit and navy tie, was clicking away on his BlackBerry, brows furrowed, eyes focused. Feeling as if we too should be engrossed in something as important, Jenn picked up a book, while I refreshed my own e-mail. The winter had left me feeling like my smartphone had become an extension of myself, constantly buzzing and ringing every time it snowed. With the snow still falling and more storms in the forecast, leaving my plow route and going on vacation seemed to add only more stress.

Upon boarding the plane, I finally gave in and powered down my computerized brain, knowing that it wouldn't work when we landed in Costa Rica. A mixture of anxiety and freedom swiftly ensued. What will I be in for when I finally do reconnect? I could picture the endless list of unread messages from my landscape clients with subject lines like: "The snow is up to the windows, when are you coming?" Or, "I can't get up my driveway, please come

ASAP." I pushed these thoughts aside, hoping my crew could handle it, and stared blankly out the window.

Jenn settled into the seat next to me, took off her glasses, and rubbed her tired eyes before continuing to read. She had had a tough winter too. Her year at work began with an assignment to a high-profile case that had her engrossed in the complexities of offshore wind energy. Stressful, day-long hearings and months of writing had imprisoned her at the office for much of the year. Unable to focus on her book, Jenn's mind wandered back to work; price suppression, electric grid reliability, and other technical topics spun in her head. Like me, she was ready for vacation but couldn't let go.

From high above the choppy waters of Boston Harbor, all of Beantown was white with snow or gray with concrete; a very depressing color pallet and one that we surely wouldn't miss. Flying south, things didn't get much better for a while. Bleak skies and barren landscapes didn't give way to sun and green until just outside Florida.

* * *

After hours of flying over open water, we finally saw land. From twenty thousand feet up, the terrain mimicked a topographic map with a hundred different shades of green bordering a turquoise ocean. Along the Caribbean coastline, miles of mangrove forest were artfully drawn upon by rivers winding to find the sea. As we flew inland, steep but soft mountains popped up, giving even more texture to the scene. Unlike a map, there were no boundaries to highlight which country we were over, but we both knew—we were back in Costa Rica.

It had all begun with Roy. Six years ago, he had mesmerized us with his stories of growing up with poisonous snakes, erupting volcanoes, and palm-tree-lined beaches. But it wasn't just his stories that had hooked us, it was how he told them. With a relaxed demeanor and a broad smile, he would always think for a second, then swing his arm and snap his fingers before starting.

"Oh man, one time, I had to pick up one of those *crazy* things to get it out of the road," he would say, talking about a sloth he came across while driving. Then, with a loud laugh, "Man, that thing was not happy with me. It was moving its legs, but rea-llll-yyyy slow, like this," he said, imitating the animal's slow movement.

Roy always made us laugh with his stories; we could hardly wait to see him in a few days.

Our plane touched down at Juan Santamaria International Airport, just outside the capital city of San José. Even before escaping the stale air of the plane, we could tell we were in a very different climate. There definitely wasn't any snow in the forecast here in tropical Costa Rica. The still-powerful late-afternoon sun penetrated the airplane's metal skin, heating up the cabin within minutes of our plane coming to a stop. Like kids ready to explore Disney World, Jenn and I stood impatiently for our turn to get off.

The airport had been modernized since our last visit. Large glass windows let in abundant natural light, and air conditioners kept the terminal cool. A plethora of flights from around the globe taxied along newly paved runways, and baggage carts buzzed between gates. Not surprisingly, the lines we remembered were the same—maybe even longer—now that more tourists were coming and going.

With our smartly packed (yet heavy) carry-on bags, we shuffled through the maze to immigration for almost an hour and then passed quickly through customs. At last, we had made it. Feeling like cattle for the better part of the day, we were finally set free, our passports now with more stamps from Costa Rica than anywhere else.

Our moment of glee was short lived. Upon exiting the airport, we were herded once again; this time by taxi drivers, tour guides, hotel representatives, and someone who seemed to be an airport official, all asking in rapid-fire Spanish if we needed transportation. We quickly declined their offers by saying, "*No gracias*," and crossed the street to a less crowded area to check our guidebook for bus information.

Obviously the painstaking Spanish lessons we had squeezed into our sixty-hour workweeks were paying off. Our instructor, Soledad, would be so proud. I could picture her grinning from ear to ear and saying, "*¡Muy bien, Matteo!*" while clapping her hands. There's nothing like learning a foreign language that makes you feel like a two-year-old.

PLANNING YOUR NEXT MOVE

You're finally in Costa Rica and are ready to start your vacation. You've claimed any checked luggage and are about to exit the airport. The ground-transportation area just outside the doors is going to be packed and chaotic. A mass of people will have their faces practically pressed against the glass looking for whoever it is they are waiting for. Before approaching this area, double check your next move, especially if you don't already have transportation arranged. Read about where to catch the bus, or if you're taking a taxi, how much it should cost to get to your destination. For more information on transportation in Costa Rica, see Appendix D.

After spending a few minutes trying to interpret the map in the guidebook, we were pointed to the bus stop by a taxi driver who had previously solicited us. "Around the parking garage and to the front," the short, brown skinned, neatly dressed gentleman said in broken English. This man was the epitome of Costa Rican friendliness, glad to take time out of his day to make sure we weren't lost.

The paved streets to downtown Alajuela, a suburb of San José, were congested with a mixture of sports cars, motorcycles, and old jalopies. Along the route, we passed everything from modern office parks, banks, and American fast-food chains to industrial facilities, hometown mechanics, and clusters of one-story residential neighborhoods. After fighting the rush-hour traffic for nearly a half hour, the bus finally dropped us off at the main station near the city center. Commuting here was just as bad as back home, except with a fresh twist, everything was in Spanish.

RIDING LIKE THE LOCALS

When visiting Costa Rica, we usually ride the public bus. We have also taken taxis, small planes, ferries, boats, rental cars, and tour vans, but buses are cheap, abundant, and dependable. Riding the bus can also get you more in touch with the local culture, something a rental car or tour van can't do.

The Tuasa, like most other buses in the San José metropolitan area, runs regularly to accommodate the large number of locals who don't have cars. We rode it from the airport to the city of Alajuela for just a couple of dollars. In most parts of Costa Rica, even rural areas, buses are common for the same reason: cars are expensive and most citizens can't afford one. Our Costa Rican friend, Roy, was always trying to buy my old Subaru station wagon when we worked together in Massachusetts. He wanted to drive it back to his hometown, a trip that would have been more than four thousand miles. To him, the trip would have been worth it. Because of import duties, a car like that would cost almost twice as much in Costa Rica.

Alajuela's central terminal was hectic with multiple bus companies competing for space under the enormous tin-roofed enclosure. Surrounding the station were blocks of two-story cement buildings with small store fronts on the ground level. These shops were packed with merchandise for the Costa Rican city dweller, each one specializing in a niche market such as electronics or clothing. Metal bars or gates ready to be closed each night protected the bounty and signaled that even in one of the world's most peaceful countries, a city is a city.

As locals swarmed the streets and sidewalks around us, we held the guidebook low, embarrassed that we didn't know which way to go. Thinking back, if the surrounding locals hadn't noticed our guidebook, they would have certainly spotted our enormous backpacks, mine bright green and Jenn's a more subtle gray but about two-thirds the size of her petite frame. There was no way to hide. Our bags were like flashing neon lights, marking us for what we really were—the equivalent of lobster-bib-wearing, duck-boat tourists in Boston.

With no street signs to guide us (typical in Costa Rica), our guidebook's detailed map was useless, so we tucked it away and decided to rely on our keen sense of direction instead.

Since we first met in a high school algebra class almost fifteen years ago, Jenn and I have been practically inseparable. Because we tend to approach life's obstacles in a similar manner, I can remember only a few serious disagreements over the years. The ones that stick out in my mind all have to do with the same thing: directions. When we are lost, the differences in our personalities are extremely apparent.

Luckily when on vacation we seldom bicker and this was no exception. Using the towering white-domed cathedral as a guide, we began walking along the narrow concrete sidewalk, knowing from previous visits that the nineteenth-century landmark was located in the city center.

The central park and cathedral grounds were a welcome change from the frantic bus station. Gardens of thick, waxy bromeliads surrounded a gurgling fountain, and neon green parakeets squawked from the tall mango trees that lined the square. The adjacent stores and restaurants served the school children, business people, and office workers enjoying the last minutes of daylight.

A block or two north of the park, we walked into Hotel Los Volcanes, a converted 1920s mansion that we had fallen in love with a few years ago. I could already envision myself settling into the luxurious room, gazing at the handcrafted woodwork, while feeling a fan wave cool air down from the twelve-foot-tall ceilings. Unfortunately, by the time we arrived, they were completely full; the comfy bed and fancy décor would have to wait. This was the risk we took by not making any reservations for our trip in advance. But for us, the flexibility to wander wherever we wanted was worth the hassle.

Not far away, down the dimly lit street, we came to a hostel that offered private rooms. The employee sitting behind a cluttered desk buzzed us through the front gate and welcomed us with a big toothy smile. The young Tico helped us with our bags and showed us the only room available: a closet-like space with twin-size bunk beds right off the main hallway, adjacent to the shared bathroom and kitchen. The room wasn't anything special, but for twenty-two dollars (about the cost of a fast-food meal for a family of four), it was a place to sleep, which was all we needed for a short night in the city.

We talked with the man for a while after putting down our bags. He wanted to hear about our travel plans and suggested some beach towns to visit from his list of favorites. He also gave us a useful city map and suggested a few places for dinner, pointing out their locations and naming their best dishes. After a long day of travel, his carefree, *pura vida* attitude was a refreshing reminder of why we love the people of Costa Rica.

TICO TERMINOLOGY

Pura vida- You may hear Costa Ricans use the term *pura vida*. *Pura vida* is a common phrase in Costa Rica, but it is also a way of life. Literally translating to "pure life," the expression is used as a greeting, a farewell, and even a way of saying that something is great. When someone is living *pura vida*, they are fully appreciating life—a good motto to live by.

Ticos and Gringos- Costa Ricans use the term Tico (masculine) or Tica (feminine) to describe a native Costa Rican, and the term Gringo to refer to North Americans or Europeans. Gringo generally does not have a negative connotation. Rather, Ticos use the term in a joking manner to describe the many foreign visitors they encounter every day. Foreigners are a normal part of daily life for Costa Ricans because of the country's heavy economic reliance on tourism. Recognizing the value that tourists bring to the country, Ticos are typically cordial and, more often than not, very friendly with tourists. So don't be surprised or upset if a Tico refers to you as a Gringo with his pals; he's just calling you what you are.

Ready to celebrate the start of our vacation, half starved, and thirsty for a drink, we sat down on a nicely landscaped patio at a nearby café. We let the heaviness of our tired bodies melt into the hand-carved wooden chairs and began to decompress. It was the first time all day that we had sat, free of our bags and the constant shuffle of travel. The night air, in the high sixties, was a little cool for our shorts and tee-shirts, but we were determined to enjoy it and forget about the frigid weather back home. We also knew that tomorrow we would be trading in this brisk mountain air for the heat and humidity of the beach that we craved.

After a relaxing dinner, we settled into our tiny closet of a room. Immediately we noticed that the walls were paper thin and a broken window let us hear everything going on in the common area and shared bathroom. As our heads hit the pillow, a German couple and a couple of hippie artists from California decided to start a lively game of cards; I think it was bridge. I don't know what was worse, the Germans trying to learn bridge or the hippies trying to speak German.

Outside the hostel, motorcycles and cars randomly throttled down the street and the occasional barking dog and hissing cat added to the intolerable soundscape. We were used to the noises of a city, but this was different. We weren't in our comfortable bed in Boston. Instead, we lay cramped in a bunk bed, listening to strangers' conversations just outside our room. Still wound up from work, our minds raced about the uncertainties of the long travel day ahead. Tossing and turning and listening to the hippies and Germans debate the rules of bridge until two o'clock in the morning, we hardly slept at all before our alarm went off at four thirty.

DAY 2

FROM CITY TO SAND

I'm so cranky," Jenn said, turning off her beeping watch.

"Mmmm . . . me too," I replied in a deep, groggy voice, hitting my head on the bunk above. "Ouch!"

The single lightbulb that hung from the ceiling burned our eyes as we zipped our bags and tied our shoes, ready to make our exit. To get revenge on our nocturnal neighbors, we made sure to make our presence known in the bathroom and let the front gate slam as we left.

The air in the valley was crisp and thin, the temperature having dropped into the low sixties overnight. In complete darkness, we scanned the streets for a taxi to take us to San José's central bus terminal, Coca-Cola. Even in the predawn hours, people were beginning to file down the sidewalks, dressed for work or school. With half-opened eyes, Jenn and I wandered like zombies among the bright-eyed Ticos before hailing the first cab we saw.

While the sun slowly rose over the emerald mountains that surround the valley, we sat miserably in the backseat of our crawling taxi, reading billboards in Spanish promoting everything from banks to fried chicken. The smell of diesel fumes wafted through the open windows and turned our hungry stomachs. Rush-hour traffic on the jam-packed, four-lane highway was barely moving, and we were nervous that we would miss the direct bus to Montezuma and be stranded for hours. But our clever driver avoided the bulk of the delay by taking an exit and maneuvering through side streets to get us to the bus station with fifteen minutes to spare.

Based on the guidebook, we expected Coca-Cola to be bustling and chaotic. The station was indeed large but surprisingly not very busy. Ten or so buses, heading in all directions, were lined up in front of and to the sides of the main building. Destination information was posted in the front window of each bus and on the wall of the building. From here it looked like you could go just about anywhere in Costa Rica. Right away we spotted the bus to Montezuma.

We stood in a short line waiting to buy our tickets alongside other tourists and locals. We passed the time talking to a young guy from California. The tall, skinny, bleach-blond surfer told us about his travel "plans": he was heading to Santa Teresa on the southwestern Nicoya Peninsula but had no idea how long he would stay or where he'd go next. Being high-strung New Englanders, we wondered how it was possible that he could leave his job and other responsibilities behind for a potentially unlimited amount of time to travel. Most importantly, we wondered how he could afford this lifestyle and if we could devise a scheme to do the same—an endless vacation in Costa Rica sounded magical.

Reality snapped back when we made it to the front of the line and had to face the bus driver. Fortunately, our Spanish seemed to pass muster and we bought our tickets without incident. After stowing our bags under the bus, we settled in for the long six-hour trip to the Pacific coast. Like a lot of public buses in Costa Rica, ours had a certain charm. It wasn't in bad condition or old, but its brown, cushiony bucket seats and yellow polyester curtains gave off a distinct '70s vibe.

SECURING YOUR LUGGAGE

If you are worried about someone taking your luggage, sit on the same side of the bus as the luggage compartment so that you can keep an eye on it when people get on and off. Usually the driver will be the one to open the compartment and help with the bags, but he will probably not keep track of to whom each bag belongs. Also, keep smaller bags and carry-ons at your seat or in the compartment directly above you, especially if they contain valuables. Most Ticos are honest, hardworking people, but just like anywhere else, there are a few bad seeds.

Two hours into our trip, we halted for a stop at a roadside snack stand and rest area. These brief stops are common for longer bus rides and allow everyone to stretch their legs, grab some food, and use the restroom. Right after we bought a couple of steaming chicken *empanadas* from a vendor's makeshift cooler, we noticed with great envy that the bus driver was eating breakfast at the *soda* next door. Although the *empanadas* were excellent, they were no *gallo pinto*, the traditional breakfast of Costa Rica that we were desperately craving and that we were sure the bus driver was eating.

WHAT IS A *SODA*?

A *soda* is the local term used to describe a no-frills restaurant that sells typical Costa Rican food and beverages. The term is used generally, so every *soda* offers something different, but they all have authentic Costa Rican dishes such as *gallo pinto* (eggs with rice and beans) and *casados* (lunch plates of fish or meat with rice and beans, a small salad, and vegetables). To drink, try the coffee for which Costa Rica is famous or, on a hot day, sip down a *refresco*, your choice of fresh fruit blended with ice or milk. Some *sodas* have seating and servers, while others are simple stands where the cook is also your server. Either way, they're a great, inexpensive way to taste the local fare.

Farm fields and overgrown pasture had dominated the landscape west of San José. But as we descended on the port of Puntarenas, the city-like feel returned. As our bus wound along the congested streets, past strips of businesses and busy sidewalks, we wondered if we'd ever get to the tropical paradise that we remembered. Then suddenly, in the crevices between the dull blocks of concrete, streaks of glimmering ocean flashed by. All that stood between us and paradise was a quick ferry ride across the Gulf of Nicoya and a short bus trip. In just a few hours, we'd be in Montezuma, exploring its raw jungle and beautiful beaches that we'd heard so much about. We couldn't wait.

Rounding a tight corner, the bus entered the ferry landing and merged into a line of tourism vans, supply trucks, and rental cars waiting to board. Small fishing boats were motoring in the bay and dock workers handled crates of fish. When we got closer to the ferry, the driver directed everyone to get off and handed us transfer tickets. Unsure if we were supposed to get our bags from under the bus or whether the bus was also coming on, we waited, watching the reactions of other travelers and the driver. Since the luggage compartment never opened and everyone just casually boarded the ferry, we did the same.

Sure enough, the bus was coming too and drove onto the massive three-story vessel a few minutes later. We were especially happy to see an Imperial beer truck not far behind. For months, we had both been dreaming of tipping back this Costa Rican favorite, and the fully loaded truck ensured an ample supply on the other side of the bay.

The ride on the ferry was slow and smooth, and the views were spectacular. Mountains surrounded the Gulf of Nicoya and small rocky islands painted with green were scattered about. We purchased two cups of coffee from the ship's cafeteria and climbed to the top deck where the view was the best. Looking over the rail, I could see schools of brown sting rays swimming away, intimidated by the mass of iron steaming toward them. Off the deck, flocks of pelicans dove for jumping baitfish, each one making a thunderous splash as it hit the water before surfacing with a stretched pouch.

While I marveled at the action, Jenn seemed content to just sit, soaking up some sun, sipping her coffee, and reading the guidebook. "Oh really?" she said when I pointed out an interesting looking boat, or, "That's nice babe," when I told her a huge fish had just jumped. But I wasn't insulted by her unenthusiastic responses. I know I tend to get overly excited about fishing and the ocean.

After about two hours of slogging across the bay, the ferry finally landed in the sleepy village of Paquera. Stepping off the boat, we took one look around and realized that we had finally escaped the city. We were in the wild of Costa Rica. To the east was an endless expanse of sparkling white and blue ocean. To the west was a blanket of rainforest brimming with tropical foliage. Strangler figs extended their shoots to suffocate competing species, wispy epiphytes clung to power lines, and broad-leafed plants occupied every inch of the rainforest floor. Struck by the land's fertility, Jenn and I couldn't help but stare in awe at our surroundings. We had seen dense forest in New England, but the biodiversity did not compare.

COSTA RICA GEOGRAPHY AND HABITATS

Biologists often tout Costa Rica as being one of the best places in the world to study wildlife—and for good reason. With four mountain ranges dividing the country's Pacific and Caribbean coasts, and one of Central America's highest peaks (Cerro Chirripó at 12,529 feet), this small country has a stunning twelve different life zones. Probably the most visited are the rainforest and highland forest zones where you can trek through jungle or cloud forest, but equally impressive for wildlife viewing are the tropical dry forest and mangrove zones.

Throughout all twelve of these zones live about 5 percent of the world's biodiversity, not bad for a country that takes up only 0.03 percent of the planet's space. The majority of Costa Rica's some 500,000 species are insects, but most tourists come to see the country's more exotic creatures like parrots, monkeys, and sloths. Scientists, on the other hand, hope to learn more about secretive or rare animals like jaguars, Baird's tapir, or Resplendent Quetzal birds. Whether you're a scientist or just a nature lover, the biodiversity you can observe within a few hours' drive from the San José airport will not disappoint.

The bus ride south from Paquera was windy and slow along a mixture of paved and gravel roads. We lumbered up steep hills and, at one point, were slowed to almost a stop when we got stuck behind a fully loaded dump truck hauling crushed stone at a snail's pace. Still in Massachusetts-driving mode, Jenn and I were about ready to take the wheel from our patient driver and show him a few tricks to resolve the situation.

"We should have passed him on that straightaway back there," I said, sighing.

"I know, or he should pull over and let us go by."

Finally we passed the truck at the top of the hill and picked up some speed. Jenn and I were sure our driver would give the guy some type of rude hand gesture as we passed (common in Boston) but, as if to mock us, he gave a friendly wave instead. Remembering that Costa Ricans take things a little slower, Jenn and I leaned back in our Burt Reynolds–style bucket seats and tried to do the same.

Gradually the thick jungle gave way to farm fields and a few small villages. Before long, we caught glimpses of the Pacific Ocean once again and rolled to a stop in Montezuma. Having picked a few hotels from our guidebook, we followed the one main road past the center of town to the first one, Hotel El Tajalin. The woman at the desk was very friendly and the hotel was nice, but the only rooms available had twin beds and cost fifty dollars per night. Having had our fill of twin-size beds the night before, we decided to keep looking.

"Do you need a room?" a friendly, soft voice asked as we were standing on the steps, contemplating where to go next.

"Ummm . . . yeah," I said, looking up.

The voice had come from Carlos, the owner of the adjacent hotel, Hotel Montezuma Pacifico, which wasn't listed in the guidebook. Nervously fumbling with his keychain, he showed us a simple but clean room with a private bath, hot water, air conditioning, a safe, and a spacious queen-size bed for forty-five dollars a night. It seemed quiet—important after our sleepless night in Alajuela—and the room was nice enough, so we booked one night, hoping to test it out before committing to more. I was especially excited to see a small lounging area that faced the quiet, well-manicured grounds of a charming church.

* * *

Overdue for lunch, we entered a casual restaurant one block away on the corner of the beach. We were enticed by the tiki-hut-style, open-air building and upbeat Latin music. Sitting at a table overlooking the water, we slowly started to forget about the day and a half of grueling travel. Instead we focused on the simmer of waves and clear blue sky that blended into the ocean; it finally felt like we were on vacation. Other tourists, mostly young people in their twenties and thirties, filled the tables around us. We could tell by their tanned skin and number of empty Imperials that they had been in Costa Rica for a while. Jenn looked down at her pasty legs and stated the obvious, "We've got some work to do."

We took a long walk on the beach and worked on our tans, although it hardly felt like work at all. Soft sand crept between our toes and we finally dipped our feet into the warm Pacific. The water was a balmy seventy-eight degrees—far warmer than the Atlantic ever gets in New England. A fresh, salty breeze cooled our wet feet and legs as we walked along the nearly deserted beach. We passed only a few surfers napping alongside their boards, resting up for another round.

Our reward for a long day of travel

Montezuma was proving to be everything we had dreamed of. So far, we had been welcomed by our friendly but shy hotel owner and had had a relaxing afternoon. Now as afternoon transitioned into night, we sat at a cozy restaurant, just steps from the beach. A gentle breeze made candles flicker and palm fronds rustle as we sipped our Caipirinha cocktails. The muddled lime and sugar balanced the strength of the powerful Brazilian liquor, and our glasses sweated in the hot night air. It was hard to imagine that just last week, I had been trapped in the cab of my truck, pushing piles of snow for thirty hours straight only to come home to Jenn, wrapped in her down coat, scraping ice from the sidewalk. The breeze blew again and we took another sip. We could get used to this.

DAY 3

AMBITIOUS ANTS WE COULD RELATE TO

The aroma slipped under our door and snaked its way to my nose.

"Is that coffee?" I whispered, getting a smile from Jenn, her eyes closed and head buried in the pillow.

We followed the scent to the Costa Rican coffee that Carlos was brewing in the lobby. We took two steaming cups back upstairs and sipped them slowly on the open-air porch. In a large mango tree nearby, a two-foot-tall Magpie Jay landed, making the branches flex. Looking at the magnificent royal-blue-and-white bird made us realize once again how lucky we were to be relaxing in warm sunshine, in February. After our last two frantic mornings, the peacefulness of just sitting there was like heaven.

* * *

Bound for the beach, we packed a bag and ambled out of our room. Just as we passed the church, we heard someone calling, "¡*Pregunta, pregunta!*"

We looked back to see Carlos trotting down the street, even his yelling was soft and relaxing. When he caught up to us, he explained his "question": he needed to know if we would be staying longer. We had neglected to tell him that we loved his hotel and that our worries of another sleepless night were unwarranted. We would definitely be staying a couple of more nights.

Tromping across fluffy white sand and over sun-bleached driftwood, we headed north. Our guidebook said that it was possible to snorkel in the tide pools in that direction, if the tide was right. Over the course of our walk, we passed several outcroppings of volcanic rock that lured us in with pooling water. Inevitably, each time we put on our masks, violent waves would start crashing. Before we knew it, four hours had passed.

"Is this going to be another chapter in the adventures of Jenn and Matt?" I asked Jenn.

"It is typical for us, isn't it?"

Many people might give up after an hour or less when trying to accomplish something, but we are notoriously stubborn. Sometimes we even drag others into our harebrained plans. A good example is when we told Roy we wanted to see a waterfall on one of our visits a few years back. Roy said he knew of one nearby but couldn't quite remember how to get there. Jenn and I encouraged him, saying that even if we didn't find it, it would still be fun to explore. Being the type of person who is up for anything, Roy went along with our plan.

On a couple of borrowed motorcycles, we took off for the mountains near Quepos, where Roy grew up. The motorcycle ride was an adventure in itself; Jenn had never been on a bike before and was terrified the entire time. She held my waist with all her strength as I drove up and down the mountainous back roads, cliffs dropping off on each side.

When we reached the end of the road and couldn't go any farther, Roy stopped and dismounted his bike. Looking in the distance toward the forest, he said, "I think this is the trail. . . . Yeah I think so. Let's go guys!"

We could tell that Roy wasn't sure we were in the right place, but we had made it this far, so we kept going. Hiking down the steep trail in old sneakers, Jenn and I were slipping and sliding along the wet orange clay and fallen leaves. Roy somehow still led the way, even in flip-flops.

After another grueling hour skidding down the mountain, we finally came to the edge of a clearing. Through the thick greenery, we could hear water gushing and feel a cool mist that hung in the heavy air. Then we saw it: a thirty-foot waterfall.

When we reached the top, Roy ripped off his shirt. Looking at us with a grin, he said, "Okay guys, we made it. It was nice to know you." Then he jumped. With some hesitation, we followed.

We recharged our tired bodies at the waterfall, repeatedly trekking to the top and jumping into the temperate water below. Verdant overgrown ferns and moss-covered rocks encased the powerful falls. Clear water swirled in a natural pool before turning back into a river. Along the rocky edges, sturdy liana vines hung from trees and made for the perfect Tarzan swing. As we swam, small silver fish brushed our legs, prompting an occasional squeal from Jenn. However, most memorable of all was that there was no one else in sight; no long lines of tourists waiting for their turn, just me, Jenn, and our good friend Roy.

That day, we were rewarded for our efforts and determination, but our adventures don't always turn out that way. Today looked like it would be a disappointment; there was no snorkeling to be found along the beaches of Montezuma. But just as we were thinking our efforts were for naught, we spotted something on the edge of the sand.

A weathered plaque stood surrounded by dozens of delicately balanced rock cairns. Visitors to the site had constructed these makeshift statues to honor some of Costa Rica's first environmentalists, Karen Mogensen and Nicholas Olof Wessburg, a Dutch-Swedish couple who settled near Montezuma in the early 1960s. These courageous people were extremely influential in shaping Costa Rica's early conservation efforts, helping to create the country's first nature reserve, Reserva Natural Absoluta Cabo Blanco. It was this reserve that led to Costa Rica protecting almost a quarter of its land from development.

We stood there for a few minutes, imagining the uphill battle that these two had endured. At the time, the Costa Rican government was focused on economic expansion, so preservation was far from the minds of those in power. Despite resistance, Mogensen and Wessburg persevered, and a national park system was eventually established. Tragically, Wessburg was later murdered in a similar quest to preserve another tract of land—Corcovado National Park—one of our favorite places in Costa Rica. Standing on the pristine beach with the virgin rainforest around us, we were taken aback by their courage to fight for something that was so unpopular, but in retrospect, so obviously right.

COSTA RICA'S NATIONAL PARKS

Since Cabo Blanco became Costa Rica's first nature reserve in 1963, Costa Rica has significantly expanded its conservation efforts and now has one of the most extensive park systems in the world. There are thirty-two national parks, thirteen forest reserves, eight biological reserves, and fifty-one wildlife refuges. Although the park system is vast, encompassing about 25 percent of the country, Costa Rica still suffers from deforestation. Like many countries seeking economic growth, Costa

Rica has been forced to balance conservation with development, which often leads to the clear-cutting of delicate ecosystems. Nonetheless, Costa Rica touts itself as an ecotourism destination, and the government seems to appreciate the value—both intrinsic and financial—of preserving the environment. After all, where else in the world can you see not just one but five active volcanoes (Arenal; Poás; Irazú; Rincón de la Vieja; Turrialba), watch sea turtles hatch right before your very eyes (Tortuguero National Park; Las Baulas Marine National Park; Ostional National Park), and hike in misty cloud forests (Monteverde Cloud Forest Reserve; Chirripó National Park)?

After a long day in the sun, the only thing we wanted to do was eat good food and recuperate. So for dinner, we happily sat down and sifted through the Italian specialties at Tairona, one of the more casual restaurants in Montezuma. I ordered a unique pizza topped with ham, hearts of palm, and an over-easy egg, and Jenn had homemade pasta Bolognese, which she raved about.

As we sipped the house-specialty cocktail of lemonade mixed with rum, we watched an endless line of leaf-cutter ants carry tiny white flowers and leaves along a concrete railing. The ants were great entertainment, especially the more ambitious ones hauling much larger pieces than the rest of the group, zigzagging and bumping into obstacles under the extra weight. These industrious ants were apparently unaware of Costa Rica's *pura vida* attitude, working long hours into the night. We could relate. Although we had begun to unwind today, our hectic jobs were still fresh in our minds. Much like us, these ants tried to carry too much and juggle too many tasks.

Putting things in perspective, the cooks roared with laughter from the kitchen. The dining room had them scrambling to make more sauce, but they were enjoying every minute. As they opened an enormous can of tomatoes, one of them sang, while the other two swayed and danced. Maybe the secret to a less stressful work life was to have a good attitude? Although I'm not sure dancing through my landscaping clients' yards would go over too well.

On the way back to our hotel, we stopped at the grocery store in town. We needed some aloe for our sunburns (so much for the tan) and drinks for the refrigerator. Although the store was modest in size, its shelves brimmed with a great variety of items. Aisles of products from fruits and vegetables to pots and pans to towels and sandals were evenly spaced and organized. Jenn, as usual, was distracted by the selection of cheeses and sent me off to find the aloe.

In my search, I picked up a notebook and a few pens, having the crazy idea to record the details of our trip so that maybe someday we could share them with the world. Before I could think too much about it, Jenn came barreling around the corner with a full basket of food and supplies, catching me with one hand in the beer cooler.

"Did you get the aloe?" she questioned.

I quickly juggled the frosty six-pack to show her that I had, smiling triumphantly.

Back at the room while sipping a beer, I began writing. A lot had taken place in the last few days and I knew that I needed to record the details before the memories were lost. Long into the night, I scribbled down what we had experienced since leaving home. As I reflected on the transition from work to vacation, I began to realize that writing would be a therapeutic escape from the stress that still wound inside me. It had been two full days without e-mail, cell phones, or really any connection to our lives and jobs back home. It was refreshing, at least the work part. Jenn, obviously already decompressed, was asleep in a flash.

DAY 4

MATING RITUALS, RARE BIRDS, AND SOME REAL HOWLER MONKEYS

At a mini-super convenience store, Jenn eyed me from an adjacent aisle.

"I don't know about those," she said, noticing my choice of some not-so-healthy-looking pastries.

"Yeah, I don't know either, but the nutrition facts are all in Spanish," I countered, easily translating the numbers on the back of the package. "Calories don't count on vacation anyway, right?" I added, watching Jenn pick out a banana to go with her yogurt. I grabbed a banana too, reasoning that one would cancel out the other.

Flakes of pastry were already flying from my face when we got to the bus station a few minutes before eight fifteen.

"Is this the bus to Cabo Blanco Nature Reserve?" I asked the driver of a parked bus, already knowing the answer from the clear label on the front.

"*No, ocho*," he replied, tapping his watch and shrugging his shoulders, looking sorry for us.

"Shoot, we missed it," Jenn said. "The guidebook said eight fifteen."

Luckily, we weren't alone; another couple from the United States had missed it as well. Since there wouldn't be another bus for a couple of hours, Jenn suggested splitting a cab with them.

"Yeah, sure, if we wait for the next bus, we'll barely have any time to hike," the twenty-something woman said.

Seven thousand Costa Rican colones (about fourteen US dollars) and twenty minutes later, a taxi dropped our foursome off at the park entrance where we each paid a small entry fee and chatted with the friendly park ranger. To be fair, he talked to us in Spanish and we understood some of it.

I pointed to a jaguar on a wildlife chart and asked, "Do these live here?" I understood from his answer that a few months ago, one was sighted close to the ranger station at night. The ranger then pointed to some other big cats but again explained that they are mostly active at night and we probably wouldn't see any.

"Well at least we won't be mauled," I said, getting a questionable look from Jenn as she looked over her shoulder at the dense forest.

We took a minute to sign into the guestbook, while the other couple headed to the trail. Curious about the other visitors, we peeked at the names. Many were from the United States or Canada, but European countries such as Germany and France were also well represented. We weren't surprised. Throughout our trips to Costa Rica, we've met people from all around the world.

The trail started off flat but climbed several steep inclines. Gigantic trees, many at least six-feet wide, were dotted throughout the forest among countless smaller varieties all stretching up, competing for the sun, and providing a shady canopy below. One of the large trees was completely hollowed out and labeled with a sign reading *"El Murciélago."* Cautiously I crept closer and looked in to see dozens of furry bats hanging upside down staring back at me with their beady eyes. A little startled, I quickly snapped a picture for Jenn, who was keeping her distance, and ran away, glad that my flash didn't set these presumably bloodthirsty creatures into a frenzy.

The park was by no means crowded but along the way we did meet some other people. Typical of travelers in Costa Rica, they were all easy to talk to and had some interesting stories and world-travel advice. One older couple was keen on birding and shared stories of the many different species they had seen. They were surprised and impressed when Jenn spotted two small black birds hopping and dancing over one another on a nearby branch on the forest floor. The elaborate mating ritual, which lasted about five minutes, was like something you would see on the Discovery Channel with feathers moving in all directions—very risqué.

Further into the hike, it was my turn to spot something strange. "Are those people wearing Red Sox hats?"

Sure enough, they were. It was a family from Boston, and it turned out that they lived in a neighborhood very close to us. While Jenn talked to the young mom about life in Boston, I talked to six-year-old Sam and his dad. Sam actually did most of the talking. He was fascinated by the howler monkeys' loud calls and would cutely bang on his tiny chest trying to imitate them. After a short chat, we let them pass so that we could take some pictures. Just as we were about to get an amazing shot of a Slaty-tailed Trogan, the bird suddenly flew away, scared off by a strange sound: Sam's dad had joined in on the howler imitations. Letting out bellowing roar after roar, his calls echoed through the forest. If he wasn't so pasty white and just a little hairier, he might have even been believable. This spectacle continued off and on for another grueling hour of our hike. Just when we thought we couldn't take any more awkward grunts, we heard the soothing swoosh of waves through the trees.

From the southernmost point on the Nicoya Peninsula,

we took in the spectacular view of the cove. Haze lifted off the ocean's cerulean waters. To our backs, steep hills brimmed with vegetation that abruptly met the palm and almond trees growing below. In the distance to the south stood a tall island with sharp cliffs, Isla Cabo Blanco. Even from far away, we could see the hundreds of nesting Brown Booby seabirds swarming.

After the long two-hour hike in the steamy rainforest, we were both drenched with sweat and ready for a swim. I peeled off my sticky shirt and jumped in first but found out the hard way that the beach dropped off into chest-deep water with a rocky bottom. Seeing me crawl back onto the sand like a walrus while being pummeled by waves, Jenn was not interested at all.

"That looks horrible!"

She was right; a sand-and-rock-filled bathing suit is not the most comfortable thing, but the water was still refreshing. Unfortunately, for the second time on this trip, we had carried our snorkel gear with us for hours and wouldn't be able to use it.

DANGEROUS WATERS

Riptides, sharp rocks, and powerful waves can really ruin a day at the beach. Although Costa Rica has its share of rough waters, a little common sense and some research go a long way. Read your guidebook to find calmer, less dangerous beaches or ask the locals before venturing into the water. Always swim with a buddy or in areas with people nearby. If you do get caught in a riptide, don't try to swim directly against it as you will become exhausted. Instead, swim parallel to the shore, angling your body toward the land. Even though some of Costa Rica's beaches aren't safe to swim, plenty are, and some of the more popular tourist destinations even have lifeguards.

Instead of swimming, we did the next best thing and parked ourselves under the shade of an almond tree. While dozing, a large chestnut-colored bird with long, black-and-white-striped tail plumage landed in the tree above us. Jenn slowly pulled out her bird book and quietly flipped the pages. Our new friend was a Squirrel Cuckoo. Like a squirrel, this bird runs and jumps from branch to branch, without opening its wings. As if on cue, it leaped to the ground so quickly that it seemed to have fallen, making a loud crunching sound as it landed on a pile of scorched leaves. Although we were stunned, the bird wasn't at all fazed and just went about its business of prodding through the leaves in search of insects.

After a good rest in the shade and some lunch, we packed up and hit the trail again. The hike back was even better for wildlife, as we made sure to leave before most of the others did, especially Sam and his noisy dad.

Climbing the steep hill from the beach, we heard something crashing through the woods, breaking twigs and rustling leaves.

"Wait," I whispered, stopping and scanning the jungle, wondering what was coming our way.

"It sounds kind of big," Jenn said, her eyes wide.

Then we saw them: a whole family of peaceful coati. As a group, the small, raccoon-like animals with long, cat-like tails were making quite a racket. The ten or so of them rummaged past us along the forest floor, turning over logs and digging with their front paws and long snouts for food, undisturbed by our presence.

Trekking back to the ranger station, we were impressed with the diversity of life we had seen in the park: the beady-eyed bats, gentle coatis, mating birds, brawny howler monkeys, a bird that acted like a squirrel, and of course Sam and his dad—a couple of "real" howlers. But the show didn't end there. On our walk to the bus stop, we saw even more amazing wildlife. A Turquoise-browed Motmot bird flaunted its electric-blue-and-black tail with racket-shaped tips in a nearby tree. Mother white-faced capuchin monkeys with their infants nestled on their backs scampered across a power line. And stealth whiptailed lizards dashed from their roadside sunning spots into the leaves. Watching the abundant wildlife, we thought back to those pioneers, Karen Mogensen and Nicholas Olof Wessburg, who were so pivotal in establishing Cabo Blanco. Without their foresight fifty years ago, this 1,172 hectare tract of land would probably be just another development on the Nicoya Peninsula. To think that all this raw, natural beauty may not exist.

A real howler monkey

At the bus stop, everyone from the trail gathered. Our wildlife show had come to an end but the entertainment continued. Two young Tico boys flew past on bicycles, showing us their best tricks (no hands!). Sam and his parents were impressed by the youngest Tico who could ride without training wheels at five years old, and so were we. Effortlessly, the boy rode back and forth across a small bridge, laughing and waving his hands in the air to show off. Dressed in only a pair of Spiderman undies, this little guy with flowing Tarzan hair and toothpick figure was quite a hoot. He was even willing to share, but when Sam had his turn, he quickly remembered that he needed the extra wheels and gave up.

Sam's dad went over to help but became distracted; Tarzan boy's mom was coming down the hill. Sam's dad, who was fluent in Spanish, greeted her. The beautiful Tica with her gorgeous matching hair told him that the boys were on school vacation, going back the following week. She then told the boys to be careful on the bikes, no riding without hands.

As the proud mom walked back up the hill, Sam's dad caught a little heat from his wife. "Geez hun, you look a little flushed after talking to that babe, you okay?" she asked.

"What? Was she attractive?" he said, while turning bright red.

"Uh yeah, she was hot!" the wife said, getting a chuckle from everyone.

Moments later, the bus came around the bend, sparing the poor guy any further embarrassment. When I stepped on, I realized that we didn't have enough small change for the fare, thanks to our unexpected taxi ride. The driver said that he couldn't break our twenty-dollar bill, so we weren't sure what to do. With no cabs much less a pay phone in the area, the seven-mile walk back to Montezuma would have been arduous after a full day of hiking. Very graciously, the family from Boston came to our rescue and helped us with the extra dollar we needed.

THE WISDOM OF MAKING FRIENDS

During our travels, we have found ourselves in quite a few jams. We have managed to get out of most of them, often because of the generosity of others. The dollar-short-for-the-bus predicament is one example. Another is avoiding a three-plus-mile walk home from a beach near Puerto Jiménez in a monsoon-like rainstorm because a nice Italian couple offered us a ride. We had met the couple on the beach earlier, when they were trying to free up their rental car from the deep sand. We helped them dig and push it out using some nearby palm fronds to keep the tires from spinning. After parting ways, they saw us walking and offered us a ride to town just before the rain came pouring down. Traveling in any foreign country presents unexpected situations that you may not be able to handle on your own. You never know when you're going to need someone's help and it's always a good idea to have people on your side.

DAY 5

SPEEDBOATS AND
SPARE BEERS

The Tylenol bottle sounded like a rattle in the quiet of morning as I clumsily shook it, trying to find relief from a hangover. Jenn was still asleep but now stirring under the covers.

The night before had been perfect, or so I thought until now. It was the type of night you can barely pry yourself away from and go to bed. It began just after sunset at one of the high-end hotels on the beach. On the tiki-torch-lit patio, we enjoyed some tropical cocktails and spring rolls, while listening to a band play soft bolero ballads. Tall palms and only a few other couples surrounded us, making the atmosphere romantic and relaxed. The air was warm, a breeze off the ocean bringing a salty freshness. Spellbound by this nearly perfect setting, we didn't want to leave. We split an entrée for dinner, intending to go after that, but when the band switched to rhythmic salsa beats, we ordered another cocktail. We lingered until the band finished its set, energized by the music and alcohol.

After drinking far more than we ate, we moved on. The party atmosphere continued in the street with hippies, surfers, tourists, and locals walking between the bars and restaurants. Cars and motorcycles occasionally rumbled through, while a group of Rastafarian bongo players filled the night air with constant drumming. Going with the beat, some scantily clad young women danced by their sides. The voices and music blended into a cacophony of sound, giving off a buzz of excitement.

We slipped in and out of a few bars, drinking Imperials at each one and talking loudly over the music to some backpackers. The young trio had story after story of the hostels where they had stayed and the interesting people they had met. We shared our disastrous experience at the hostel in Alajuela, and they laughed.

After a while, we stumbled back to our hotel, the drinks making things more than a bit foggy. The sound of bongos and rock music grew faint as we closed the wide wooden door of our room. Little did we know the rhythm of pounding bongos still would be throbbing in our heads when we awoke.

"I'll take one of those too," Jenn grumbled, putting her palm out.

Nursing our hangovers with some of Carlos's coffee, we reflected on our stay in Montezuma. When planning our trip, we weren't sure that we wanted to take the time to visit this somewhat difficult to access town. But by the end of our stay, we had fallen in love with its energetic yet relaxed vibe, eclectic restaurants, and beautiful scenery. Resolving to someday return, we reluctantly packed our belongings and said goodbye to Carlos and Montezuma.

* * *

From the edge of the beach, Jenn and I waited for the boat that would take us to Jacó on the main coast. From Jacó, we planned to continue south by bus to Quepos and Manuel Antonio to see Roy. Expecting a ferry, we were surprised when a small speedboat pulled ashore. The boat was about twenty-feet long and its shallow berth didn't look very stable. Jenn glanced at me, looking green. Despite our queasy stomachs, we splashed through the shallow water and found our seats beside the dozen other passengers.

"Cross your fingers," Jenn said, as she gauged the distance from her seat to the side of the boat.

"We'll be fine," I countered, gauging for myself the best way to hurl over the side.

Fortunately, the ride was much smoother than we had expected. Thanks to the power of our boat's hefty outboard engine, we were propelled out past the turbulent waves and into the glimmering bay before anyone could think about losing their breakfast. With just a few splashes of water making it into the boat, we raced past Tortuga Island and crossed the wide Gulf of Nicoya to Jacó.

When we arrived, the beach was crowded with tourists and locals, swimming, barbequing, or just soaking up the sun. Jacó beach is an easy trip from San José, and since it was the last weekend of school vacation, Tico city dwellers were taking full advantage of what free time they had left. Dodging one wave after another and swimmers scattered about, our captain timed the waves perfectly and effortlessly landed the boat on the shore.

* * *

A beach landing in Jacó

Thankful to be back on terra firma, we loaded into a tourism van and were driven to the bus station a few miles down the road. We waited for the bus at the smoldering stop for almost two hours, dripping sweat in the intense midday sun. When the Quepos bus finally rounded the corner, it was completely full. Locals overflowed from the seats into the aisles. Luckily, the driver opened the back door and let us squeeze in. I'm sure the Ticos made a few jokes about the two Gringos crouched in the handicap area, but we were oblivious, happy to be on the bus and out of the sun.

A tween-aged Tica sitting across the aisle amused us with her uncontrollable cell-phone obsession. She would giggle and take pictures of herself, then text them to some love-struck boy, all while her mother slept soundly in the seat next to her. It was apparent that Costa Rica had entered the digital age, but a relief that we hadn't set up our own cell phones to work here. Part of me, though, still wanted to grab the girl's phone and text someone back home, "How's the weather? Any problems with the SNOW?"

Riding south through Parrita and what seemed like miles of palm farms, we saw (and smelled) one of the major factories in the area. The palm factory looked similar to the paper mills we were used to seeing back home in Maine, with a large central smokestack. But instead of smelling like rotten eggs, the plant emitted a sweet, pungent odor from the palm oil it processed.

INDUSTRY IN COSTA RICA

Costa Rica has been long known for bananas and coffee, but its economy is based on more than just Dole, Chiquita, and a good cup of joe. Other crops, such as rice, sugar cane, pineapple, and oil palm, make up a large share of the country's total exports. Aside from agriculture, foreign investments have spurred thriving healthcare and technology industries in the country's major cities. Above all else, though, Costa Rica's most lucrative industry is ecotourism, the industry that shows off its most valuable resource—the country itself.

Beyond the palm factory, our bus passed through a few more sleepy towns, each marked by a collection of modest concrete-block homes that were spread out among vast farm fields and more palm forests. Occasionally, traffic came to a stop for construction crews repairing the road. Costa Rica had been hit hard during its last rainy season with repeat storms, causing landslides and washouts of many roads. After about an hour and a half, we reached Quepos.

By Costa Rican standards, Quepos is a large town. It's not quite a city in the traditional sense like San José but has an urban feel with its concentrated downtown, concrete sidewalks, and residential outskirts. Quepos is already a big sportfishing hub, and for the last few years, developers have been expanding the marina to accommodate cruise ships, which will bring more tourists to the area. The cruise ships currently stop in Puntarenas on the Pacific coast and Puerto Limón on the Caribbean coast, but some would say that Quepos is an even more desirable tourist destination with Manuel Antonio's beautiful park and beaches nearby.

The bus dropped us off at the centrally located terminal alongside half a dozen other buses. The area was crowded and hectic with people gathered around benches or shopping in the storefronts, which framed the space. A line of red taxis and tour vans waited across the street. Focused on retrieving our bags from under the bus, I stood in the scrum of passengers for my turn, while Jenn stepped to the side. Our carry-ons finally came into sight after most of the bags were claimed, and I grabbed them by maneuvering around a slower gentleman.

As I turned to find Jenn, I noticed that the crowd had quickly dispersed. A strange, panicked feeling came over me.

Seeing my eyes bulge, Jenn asked, "What is it?"

"My wallet's gone!"

Watching me frantically pat myself down like my shorts were on fire, Jenn, as usual, tried to be optimistic.

"Maybe it just fell out on the bus."

We looked for it everywhere: on the bus, in every pocket of my shorts, and on the bus again. Then it dawned on me.

"There was a guy pushing me when I was getting the bags. But how could he? He couldn't have slipped into my pocket, right?"

A few minutes passed and we stepped off the bus, defeated and confused. Was this really happening?

Then suddenly a teenager wearing a red striped polo shirt and some baggy designer jeans appeared.

"Did you lose a wallet?" he asked in a Spanish accent, holding up my small black bifold. The young Tico nonchalantly explained that he had found it lying on the ground by the bus and pointed to a spot near the back tire.

Jenn was ecstatic and proceeded to give the guy a great big hug. I, on the other hand, was more skeptical. I flipped through my now very lightweight wallet to discover that all the cash was gone. Looking closer I was slightly relieved to find my credit cards and driver's license still in place. Scattered thoughts raced through my head: Did these pickpockets have morals? Did they really just steal my wallet and give it back? And—is Jenn hugging that guy?

Whether the kid was involved or not, the thieves didn't make out with much. He did somehow manage to score a hug from my wife, but luckily I was only carrying forty dollars and the rest was hidden safely away in our bags. Although we were extremely happy that we didn't have to go through the hassle of cancelling our credit cards, we still felt a little less secure and disappointed that it had happened at all.

Pura vida . . . I guess.

PERSONAL SECURITY

Costa Rica is a very peaceful country, right down to its *pura vida* motto. Violent crimes occur less frequently than in other Latin American countries and even less often than in the United States. As our story of being pickpocketed shows, though, tourists shouldn't get too comfortable. Crime does occur, and visitors should exercise the same level of caution they would when visiting any other foreign country.

Petty theft and pickpocketing are the most common crimes against tourists. To avoid being a victim, keep your valuables secure at all times, especially your passport, travel documents, and cash. Keep your luggage close and be observant, particularly in crowded areas like bus stations, busy streets, and other places where people congregate. If you rent a car, do not leave anything inside it; theft from cars is common and thieves know which vehicles are rentals.

In the event that you are the victim of a crime, contact the local police immediately. Costa Rica takes its reputation as the safest destination in Central America seriously; you may even see the police patrolling popular tourist areas.

Keep these safety tips in mind when you travel but remember too that Costa Rica is generally safe. Other than the pickpocketing incident, we haven't experienced any crime during our travels and almost always feel safe.

With our bags on our backs (and our hands on our wallets), we easily found the bus that runs between Quepos and Manuel Antonio. Our timing couldn't have been better. Sometimes we've waited a half hour or more for this bus, but today it was right there. Much more observant now that we had been robbed, I noticed several more polo-shirt-wearing Ticos hanging around. Keeping a close eye on the alleged group of five-foot-tall, Where's Waldo thieves, we found our seats.

"If those are the guys, they're crazy!" Jenn said, eyeing the group out the window. "If you would have caught them in the act, you could have taken them out; you're at least a foot taller than all of them!"

Picturing myself behind bars in a Costa Rican jail cell, I shrugged off the thought of what could have happened and was glad things worked out the way they did. As for

Jenn, I thought I would just let her continue thinking that I could have taken the five of them out by myself.

After a quick ten-minute ride up the small mountain and down the other side, we got off the bus at a much less threatening place, the beach. Just yards from the sand, we walked along the palm-tree-lined sidewalk and stared off at the waves.

MANUEL ANTONIO

Manuel Antonio is far from lacking in hotel and dining options. Eco-lodges, hostels, as well as luxury and midrange accommodations line the steep, narrow road between Quepos and Manuel Antonio. Open-air restaurants are everywhere and provide a great variety of cuisine at moderate prices and priceless views of the jungle. You're practically guaranteed to see lizards when dining alfresco and may even see squirrel monkeys, which often come down to the restaurants on the beach around dusk. Although the area has become very built up, it hasn't lost its charm. There is still quite a bit of open land (though much of it is for sale), and the existing businesses fit into the natural environment quite nicely.

This was our third visit to Manuel Antonio, and we had a particular place in mind for accommodations. We are a bit nostalgic for the first hotel at which we stayed in Costa Rica, Manuel Antonio Hotel. Located right on the beach and near the entrance to Manuel Antonio National Park, it's in an ideal location. Unfortunately, in the spirit of our less-than-perfect day, the hotel was completely booked.

Next we tried Villa Prats, a hotel that is also near the park entrance. We walked in and were greeted by Jason, a friendly face we immediately recognized from our stay there a year ago. He remembered us too and gave me a warmhearted handshake. It was nice to see that he remembered us. We had only stayed at the hotel for a few nights, but I suppose we had been memorable guests.

What probably triggered his memory was our wake-up-call disaster. It began one night when we asked Jason to give us a wake-up call for six o'clock the next morning. We were traveling with another couple and had all booked a zip-line tour for the following day. The tour van was picking us up at seven, and we weren't sure we would wake up on our own. Jason didn't speak much English and we didn't speak much Spanish, but we tried to communicate with him in Spanish whenever possible. We were, after all, in a Spanish-speaking country and wanted to respect the native language.

Our friend Kristen, whom we relied on throughout the trip because of her good grasp of Spanish, took the lead. Although to my ear her flowing sentences sounded perfect, she had trouble communicating with Jason during our stay; she did say her Spanish was rusty. Whatever she said, Jason seemed to understand, as indicated by his nodding and smiling. But we weren't convinced. Ticos are known for their politeness, and because of this, feel the need to say yes when sometimes the answer is no, maybe, or I don't understand. To make matters worse, you will almost never find a clock, never mind an alarm clock, in a Costa Rican hotel room. To be sure that we were covered, Kristen kept her camera, which had the time, close to her pillow so she could check it if she woke up.

The next morning our peaceful slumber was hijacked by frantic knocking.

"It's quarter of seven. Wake up!" Kristen shouted.

Jenn jumped out of bed in a panic and met her at the door. She told Kristen that we would be ready in five minutes. After throwing on some clothes and barely tying our sneakers, our foursome raced down the stairs. On our way past Jason, who was casually standing near the front desk, Kristen asked him why he didn't wake us up. Obviously confused, Jason pointed to his watch while saying something in Spanish. None of us understood what he said and we didn't have time to figure it out, so we ran off to meet the van.

At seven thirty, our ride still had not arrived. We knew that the concept of time is very loose in Costa Rica (hence no clocks), but a half hour was later than normal, especially for a tourism business. Seeing that a small restaurant on the corner was opening, we asked a woman working there for the time.

"Six thirty," she replied.

Kristen had forgotten to reset her camera to account for the one-hour time change!

Laughing, we realized why Jason had been confused and later apologized. A year later, not surprisingly, he still remembered the crazy, early-rising Gringos.

After talking to Jason for a bit, we asked about a room. He told us they were full that night but had openings after that. We preferred not to change hotels midcourse, so we said goodbye, wished him well, and made our way farther down the road. As soon as we left, a local guy approached.

"Hey, you guys looking for a room?" the middle-aged, shirtless Tico said in a Cheech-and-Chong-sounding voice.

Hungry for lunch and fatigued from carrying our thirty-pound backpacks, we neglected to say *no gracias*. Before we knew it, we had a personal, although unwanted, hotel agent. Our new friend was your typical beach-bum local who knew everyone and everything about the town and had a slight odor of beer. The type that everyone says hello to but in an, oh, it's you again, sort of way. He led us around from one hotel to another, and although he did seem to know someone who worked at each one, it was soon clear that he had no idea which had vacancies and which didn't. He was really nice and chatty, so it was hard to get rid of him. But after his third attempt to sell us on a hostel when we said we wanted hot water and air conditioning, Jenn, hungry, hot, and getting increasingly impatient, shot me a look that said she was not putting up with this for much longer. I had seen this look before and knew I had to do something fast. I quickly dug into the bottom of my backpack and pulled out a lukewarm Imperial left over from Montezuma.

"Thanks for helping us, but we can find something on our own," I said, holding out the beer in a peace offering.

"Wow, thanks," the guy replied, not wasting any time to crack it open. And with that, our unwanted friend turned on his bare heel and went off in the other direction as if the last half hour had never happened.

At a hotel farther up the hill, we tried our luck again. When we walked into the office of Hotel Coco Beach, the owner offered us a room at her new luxury hotel down the street for $200 a night. We were shocked; I had to look twice to make sure she wasn't wearing a striped polo and trying to steal my wallet.

"Our budget is more like fifty," I said.

"Well, how long do you want to stay?" the older Asian woman asked.

"Two nights."

Looking down at her reservations' book, she paused for a moment, squinting her eyes, and said, "I have one room available here. It's seventy dollars a night as long as you stay two nights *and* pay cash."

"Okay," I said, smiling and looking at Jenn for the cue that she too was okay with the price.

"Lupiiiiiitaaaa!" the woman shouted out the front door. "Show these people 6B right away."

Lupita, a young woman from housekeeping, whisked us up four steep flights of concrete steps before we reached the building highest on the hill. Huffing and puffing, I caught my breath while the unaffected ladies opened the massive wooden door. Jenn had a major cardio advantage over me with her frequent trips to "spin class," and Lupita could be nicknamed "The Stairmaster" with her daily routine of up and down.

"Wow," Jenn said, stepping into the room. "There are three double beds!"

"And look at that view," I said, taken aback by the stunning cove below. Around the corner, past a nice sitting area, was a large pool and hot tub. There was no doubt that we were booking this place; it was amazing.

On top of our private mountain, we jumped between the hot tub and pool, sipping from cans of cold beer. Covered to our necks in warm, bubbly water, we let ourselves do nothing but relax, altogether forgetting about the stress of our daily lives. Sure, we could have checked our e-mail in the hotel lobby or even at one of the Internet cafés, but we didn't. We didn't want to. If vacation were some kind of twelve-step program beginning with buying your plane ticket and ending with a complete revitalization of your soul, we were somewhere in the middle. Let's say step five, getting in a hot tub and forgetting that you sometimes wear shoes.

* * *

Our destination for dinner was El Avión, an old camouflage cargo plane that was converted into a restaurant. It is a landmark in Manuel Antonio and for good reason. The food is decent and reasonably priced for the area, but the atmosphere is what makes it special. The bar area where we dined is inside a plane connected to the Iran-Contra Affair.

During the midst of the Cold War in the mid-1980s, the US government covertly provided military aid and support to the Contras, a group of Nicaraguan insurgents who were trying to overthrow Nicaragua's Sandinista government. The aid included two identical Fairchild C-123 cargo planes, one of which was shot down in 1986 en route to deliver supplies to the Contras. After the Sandinistas' successful strike on the C-123, the US government aborted the operation and abandoned the remaining plane at Costa Rica's San José international airport.

In 2000, the owners of El Avión purchased the C-123 for $3,000 and had it disassembled, shipped to Quepos, and reassembled into the restaurant that exists today. The army relic, which sits as if it crashed into the hillside, seems especially out of place in a country that has been without a standing military since 1948. After all, Costa Rica is known for its monkeys and not guerillas.

After a light dinner and a couple of drinks, we climbed into the cockpit, honing our piloting skills, before navigating back down the hill to our hotel. It had been another long day of travel, but we had made it back to the place where we fell in love with Costa Rica. And even though Manuel Antonio had changed since our first visit, it hadn't lost its appeal. We may have had to share it with more tourists and pay slightly higher prices, but its captivating beauty was still the same. It was good to be back.

DAY 6

CLEVER MONKEYS AND
RAGING BULLS

Light poured in through the crack above the door. I could hear the distant thundering of waves as they crashed and sizzled on the beach below. Outside the window, a bird began to whistle. If these sounds weren't enough to wake me from my peaceful slumber, the noise of Jenn fervently turning the pages of the guidebook certainly was. As I rolled over and opened one eye, I was suddenly grilled with questions about our plans for Uvita and Drake Bay from my chipper wife who had been awake and researching for an hour already, very uncharacteristic.

Jenn was having second thoughts about our decision not to make reservations for lodging. She was uneasy because it had been difficult for us to find a hotel in Manuel Antonio, and our next two destinations farther down the Pacific coast were smaller and would likely have fewer options. She probably also didn't feel like being dragged around town again by a shirtless guy who gets paid in beer.

Having just opened my eyes, I wasn't ready for such an intense discussion but agreed that we should probably make reservations for Drake Bay just to be safe. We didn't think we'd have a problem finding accommodations in Uvita, but from the details in our guidebook, it seemed logical for Drake Bay, a much more remote location.

At a pay phone on the beach, we tried to get our phone card to work. A young woman working at a nearby store must have seen our frustration because eventually she came over to help. Apparently when making local calls from a pay phone, you need to press a certain number combination before entering the number you wish to call. We later discovered that, no, the elusive combination was not some secret code known only to Ticos. All I had to do was select the option for English, and the operator would have provided instructions.

But in our defense, you had to have a solid understanding of Spanish even to figure out that the phone had an option for English, and we didn't. In fact, on the last day of our Spanish class when asked to explain what I like to wear in the summer, I answered, *"Una falda."*

"¿Una falda?" Soledad questioned, the corners of her mouth turning up in a smile. "Does Matteo like to wear a skirt in the summer?"

With that, the class began roaring with laughter, while I turned as red as a tomato. Cheating off your wife's Spanish workbook is not always the best idea.

With the help of our pay-phone tutor, we called a lodge in Drake Bay and booked a reservation. The host made sure we knew how to get there and said he would arrange a water taxi for us.

"A guy will find us in Sierpe at this place called Las Vegas and take us over on his boat. I guess there are no good roads," I said, as I hung up the receiver.

"That's great. Who is he and how will he know who we are?"

"Hmm, I don't know. He didn't say. I'm sure it'll be fine though."

Jenn wasn't so sure and neither was I, really, but we were both learning that things in Costa Rica are extremely laid-back and, truth be told, it probably would work out. Feeling better about our plans, we grabbed a quick breakfast and headed to the entrance of Manuel Antonio National Park.

EXPLORING COSTA RICA'S PARKS

Costa Rica has beautiful parks filled with exotic flora and fauna. To see all that the parks have to offer, take your time and keep your eyes and ears open. Guides are a great option if you haven't visited an area before. They will provide endless information on the native plants and animals and also know where to look for wildlife because they travel along the same trails every day. In addition, guides have powerful scopes that can give you a great look at a species without disturbing it.

You can book a guide through most hotels or even right outside some parks. At Manuel Antonio National Park and other popular parks, guides congregate outside of the entrance, hoping to lure in tourists who haven't booked a tour yet. Although there is true value in a knowledgeable guide, once you catch on to the basics, you can probably manage by yourself. You may even see more wildlife exploring on your own because guides usually work on a time limit, stay to a set trail, and travel with large groups that can scare off wildlife.

This was our third visit to the park, so when we finally made it through the tall gates, we skipped the hype of the guides and made a beeline to the beach. Jenn had fallen in love with snorkeling on our first trip to Manuel Antonio when I convinced her to try it at one of the beaches in the park. Little did we know that the calmness of the ocean on that particular day, which provided ideal conditions for learning, would be a rarity for us in Costa Rica. On this particular visit, the water was choppy, which made it a bit cloudy, but we still managed to see some colorful fish along the rocks. Jenn, now a pro, was more determined than me and stayed in the water longer than I had ever seen.

Back on the sand, we ate some snacks and watched angrily as what felt like one hundred tourists congregated around a troop of white-faced monkeys that had come down for handouts. The tourists oohed and ahhed as the brazen monkeys grabbed food from people's hands. This had happened on each of our visits to the park, and even though the animals can be seriously harmed and there are signs prohibiting the act, many tourists can't resist the opportunity to get close to the wildlife. The monkeys had the last laugh though. While one group distracted and entertained the tourists from a tree, another raided their unattended backpacks. The stealth monkeys unzipped the bags, chose what they wanted for lunch, and ran back to the woods with their loot. This tactic works every time, and we have even seen it executed perfectly by a savvy family of raccoons.

NO MONKEY BUSINESS

Everyone likes photographing monkeys, they can provide hours of entertainment. But feeding them to get that perfect shot can be a real danger to the animal. Contrary to popular belief, bananas are not the primary food source for these furry, long-tailed creatures, nor are potato chips or Twinkies. In fact, strange foods can cause dental and stomach problems for the adults and lead to malnourished offspring. Monkeys can also become sick, or even die, by eating foods that people have touched because they are sensitive to the bacteria on human hands. The best way to ensure you get that perfect snapshot is to keep the monkey population healthy and safe. So please, don't feed the monkeys.

On our way out of the park, we went back to our favorite pay phone to call Roy. Not doing much with his day off, Roy said he would come over to the beach for a swim and told us that he would like to take us to a festival that night in Parrita.

Jenn had had enough swimming for one day, her snorkel-mask outline still imprinted on her face, so when Roy showed up, he and I grabbed a couple of beers and walked down to the beach by ourselves. It was great to catch up with my good friend and share stories of what had happened in the year since we had last seen each other. Roy was doing great. He had recently bought a car and had even taken out a loan for a piece of property nearby. His job in the tourism industry was treating him well, and I couldn't have been happier for him.

As we swam, we reminisced about the time we had spent together in the States: Roy's first experiences watching the leaves in New England change color and then the snow that came shortly after. I'll never forget how excited he was to see the snow, videotaping every moment to show his family and friends back home. Most of all, though, we laughed and joked about some of the great times we shared in the landscape truck.

Roy had become a close friend very quickly; sometimes two people are compatible that way. He is the type of person who is fun loving, often a prankster, but always with the best intentions and a good heart. Roy and I could tell each other stories all day long. My favorites of his were the multiple times he crashed his bicycle or motorcycle into a river, but his stories of growing up with monkeys, sloths, and a variety of poisonous creatures were equally entertaining. My stories of growing up were less exotic, but the coast of Maine seemed to be just as interesting to my Costa Rican friend. Even though we were separated by thousands of miles, childhood memories seem to be universal.

* * *

At dusk, Roy led us through the crowded gates of the annual festival and rodeo in Parrita. We were immediately struck by how similar the fairgrounds were to those in the United States. Large barns held exhibits and temporary shops. Vendors were selling everything from sunglasses to cowboy hats to small household items. There were games, rides, tractors, and plenty of livestock, which made it smell like a fair back home too. The food was also similar but had a Tico touch. Oddly enough, we both had American-style Chinese food filled with mysterious native vegetables. Anxious to get into the arena for the bull riding, we purchased our tickets and carried in our food.

The wooden bleachers of the arena were almost full, but we managed to find a spot with a view of the gate where the bulls and riders were let out. We were surrounded by Ticos, which was strikingly different from Manuel Antonio, where we were just two of hundreds of tourists. Looking around, we began to appreciate the cultural importance of the event. There were families everywhere. Sitting next to us was a couple with two young children. They had brought along one of their parents, an elderly man in a ten-gallon hat, red plaid shirt, and shiny, silver belt buckle. With a wide grin, the grandfather would playfully grab the kids as they scrambled around, restless for the show to begin. Later, a middle-aged woman, who resembled the young mother, arrived, greeting the group with a wave. Another man came and sat down next to them, probably an uncle or cousin, then another, and another, until finally, about fifteen people had squeezed into our row. They were all of different ages, but their physical similarities and mannerisms suggested that they were related to each other in some way.

As we watched this family and the many others around us, we thought about how long it had been since our own extended families had come together. Was it for a wedding or a baby's birth? Or, sadly, was it because of someone's death? Thinking back to the shuffle of our busy lives, I realized how it seemed to be becoming more and more difficult to get everyone together. We could learn a lot from the Ticos, I thought.

Meanwhile, amidst the families, clans of teenage boys swaggered by, chasing the many young women dressed for a night out in flashy clothes and high heels. The scene was noisy with music blaring and vendors whistling to sell refreshments. We took in the sights and sounds over a couple of beers while waiting for the riders. After all of the riders were announced, there were some lengthy ceremonies and a prayer for the participants (all in Spanish) before finally the bull riding began.

In a flash, each powerful bull hurled itself out of the gate, kicking and spinning as the announcer talked louder and faster. The action was intense, and the crowd cheered as the clock ticked past. Typical for a rodeo, most riders were able to stay on the angry creatures for only a few seconds before being tossed off and pummeled with hooves and horns. But unlike any rodeo we had seen, the show didn't stop there.

Lots of spectators, many of them drunk, stood along the walls of the ring, taunting the bull while the rider retreated. At random, the bravest (or most drunk) would leap into the pit, yelling and waving his arms to antagonize the beast. As the irritated bull charged after him, dozens of hands reached from behind the fence, trying to slap or poke the animal's backside. One of these idiots misjudged his timing and was stabbed by the bull's flailing horns. As he was pulled away, his shoulder oozing blood, the crowd buzzed nervously. Finally, when enough damage was done, cowboys on horses rode out to lasso the bull and lead it to the stables before the spectacle was repeated.

A Costa Rican rodeo

The bull riding was thrilling in itself, but our night of excitement didn't end there. On the ride back to Manuel Antonio, we witnessed some of the driving habits for which Costa Rica is famous. At one point, we were passed on the right by a speeding car with no headlights and then, minutes later, had to slam on the brakes for an old truck going about as fast as a donkey. Roy displayed his own Tico style by passing the old clunker on a sharp curve while giving us both a mild heart attack.

"Here—we—go," he said, as we prayed there wasn't an oncoming car waiting around the bend. Smoothly curving back to our lane just before a set of headlights appeared, Roy acknowledged our stunned expressions with a smile. "Take it easy guys. You worry too much."

Back at the hotel, we sadly said goodbye to our dear friend Roy. It was our last night in Manuel Antonio, and we wouldn't see him for another year. Unbeknownst to him, in one short day, Roy had left a lasting impression on us. He reminded us of why we had fallen in love with Costa Rica, its friendly people and laid-back culture.

With Roy, we got to step inside the life of a Tico. Not just his, but the lives of whomever we encountered. He had done it on each of our trips, just by going about his life and bringing us along. Tonight it was the family at the rodeo, generations coming together for a night of fun and excitement. On another trip, it was Roy's young son and neighbor, sharing stories with us through translation on the balcony of Roy's apartment in a local Quepos neighborhood. And on our first trip, it was Roy's mother. She welcomed us into her home like we were family for an elaborate meal that we'll never forget. We had a unique advantage over any other tourist; someone to show us what life in Costa Rica was really like. Each of these events gave us a deeper cultural appreciation and a desire to discover more. With a renewed sense of adventure, Jenn and I were ready to explore Costa Rica's more remote towns—on our own.

DAY 7

WELCOME TO UVITA:
ARE WE THERE YET?

The bus geared away, leaving us on the side of the newly paved Costanera Sur highway in Uvita. We could have easily missed our stop if I hadn't noticed the handmade "Welcome to Uvita" sign leaning crookedly against a tree.

Described as a charming hamlet, Uvita was supposed to be a hidden gem with pristine beaches and the country's only underwater national park, Marino Ballena. Other than this brief description, our guidebook didn't offer much information. Uvita was supposed to be undeveloped, and we were fine with that. After competing for towel space on Manuel Antonio's busy beaches, we were ready for some peace and quiet. Most of all, we were excited to explore a more remote area to get a deeper sense of the culture.

As the bus rolled out of sight, we looked around. This was not the quaint village we had imagined. Straddling the highway were strip malls that housed a grocery store, two banks, a couple of pharmacies and restaurants, and some other shops. The charming *cabinas* (cabins) and small-town *sodas* we yearned for were nowhere in sight. Looking at the towering mountains to the left and farm fields to the right, and not knowing where anything was, we decided that we'd better call some hotels before setting off on foot. I spotted a pay phone.

"*Hola, Banco National de Costa Rica,*" a sweet-sounding, young Tica answered.

"Hi, I was wondering if you had any rooms?"

"*¿Que . . . ? Lo siento. No entiendo.*"

"Uhhhh . . . *¿Habla inglés?*"

A few awkward moments later, a man came on the line. "Hello, can I help you?"

"Oh hi, yes, I was wondering if you had any rooms available tonight?"

"Rooms? I'm sorry, sir, this is the national bank of Costa Rica. I think you have the wrong number."

There was a sudden click as the man hung up on me.

Gazing over the pay phone, across the street, I turned to Jenn and started to chuckle. "I just called the bank over there; they don't have any rooms."

Several more calls left us with only busy signals or no vacancies. Our guidebook options were quickly exhausted. Hoping that there was somewhere to stay near the national park, which hadn't made it into the guidebook, we started walking toward the ocean.

* * *

The sides of the dirt road were flanked with open fields of overgrown pasture. A few thirsty trees were dotted in, making the scenery look like an African savanna, dry but exotic. For about a half hour, we walked in awe of our surroundings, our conversations upbeat and enthusiastic. It was exciting to be exploring someplace new, off the beaten path and out of our comfort zones.

The charm of our surroundings, however, was not enough to sustain our good moods. We were almost living *pura vida* but weren't quite there yet, and things started to go downhill fast. Our breakfast had worn off, and the heat was beginning to take its toll. With nothing around except a few houses and some bony cattle, we began to wonder if we'd ever find a hotel.

Finally we came to an intersection. In one direction was a newly paved road. In the other was the same rough and dusty dirt we had been walking on. Perplexed, we watched numerous cars turn off the paved road onto the dirt one. After a quick debate and a bit of hesitation, we followed them, thinking there must be something worthwhile that way.

Trailing behind a slow-moving sedan as it swerved to avoid ruts and rocks, we continued down the road. After another half hour of walking in the stifling heat, our efforts finally paid off. The desert-like fields gave way to shady forest and the ocean.

In between palm trees, dozens of cars were parked on the edge of a pristine beach. The smell of charcoal and barbeque chicken wafted through the air. Children laughed and shrieked from the sand, playing soccer or splashing in waves. A kite flew. In the shade, parents lounged on blankets or sat around picnic tables. They were all Ticos. It seemed that we had found a local hot spot, either that or we were hallucinating from dehydration.

Like other points along Costa Rica's Pacific coast, Uvita's beaches feature picturesque palm trees, clean white sand, and cresting waves that cascade up and down a long coastline. But unlike other seaside towns with rolling hills that dip toward the ocean, Uvita is bordered by steep, lush mountains. Adding to the dramatic backdrop, the peaks of these majestic mountains were shrouded in a dense layer of cloud.

As we watched the relaxed Ticos and the calm azure

ocean, our moods once again mellowed. We rested for a moment, comparing ourselves to the people around us. Our lives were so different. A day at the beach seems like such a chore back home, fighting traffic, parking meters, frigid water. Never mind the crowds. What if it were more like this? Palm trees instead of parking spots and water as warm as the air. Taking in the refreshing breeze for a few more moments, we eventually forced ourselves to come back to reality. After all, we had found the beach, but still hadn't found a place to stay.

A poorly drawn map, which we had picked up at the bus stop, wasn't much help. About as detailed as a pirate's treasure map, it consisted of dotted lines and crudely penciled landmarks. Up until now, we had seen only one or two abandoned motels, a scattering of houses, and a few horses, so we didn't have a lot to go by. But by cross-referencing the map with the guidebook, we determined that we were at the free entrance to the park (hence the locals). If we wanted to get to the village center, where we thought there were hotels and restaurants, we needed to walk north toward the main (Gringo) entrance.

A shaded trail paralleling the ocean led us onto the beach and eventually to the gates of the park entrance. We made our way toward them but became distracted by something in the distance. There was a long, narrow point stretching almost a kilometer into the ocean. Near the tip, it widened into a dramatic fan-shaped sandbar. This was Uvita's famed whale tail. Even from the beach we could see its shape. A perfect tail formed by the converging currents of two adjacent coves. It was only fitting that out past this sandbar in the deeper water is where several species of whale, including the humpback, come to breed.

Uvita's whale tail

We walked back to the official entrance to the park, passed through the gates, and found the other end of the elusive paved road. Finally, the archaic treasure map, with all its incomprehensible markings, made sense. Tears streamed down our sweaty faces as we doubled over, laughing at the realization that we had taken the longest possible route to Playa Uvita.

The immediate area had a few *sodas*, a handful of brightly colored stucco homes, and some other small businesses. The streets were quiet, the sound of waves from the ocean still audible in the distance. A pair of chickens from a house across the street grazed past along the edge of the road. Lots of locals were walking around: a man with a bag of groceries smoking a cigar, a couple of older women out for a stroll, and a young woman holding her baby. They all cast us a friendly glance. School children in navy slacks and white dress shirts congregated in front of a mini-super, kicking a soccer ball.

Jenn looked at me and smiled. This was it: the Ticos, the beach, the tranquility, the culture. We had finally found the quaint village we were looking for. It might not have been perfect for everyone, but it was for us.

* * *

At Dagmar, a small motel hidden away off the main road, we settled into our room. It was far from luxurious but covered the basic necessities and was only thirty dollars a night. Lounging on the cushiony recliners on our porch, we soaked up the afternoon. Jenn wrestled a tough local *limón* that we picked up at one of the mini-supers in town until every drop of juice was squeezed from its bright orange flesh onto a ripe avocado. We enjoyed this fresh guacamole with some ice-cold beer.

As we kicked back, brightly colored birds cruised by. In streaks of blue, yellow, and green, tanagers, Gray-capped Flycatchers, and lots of tiny hummingbirds glided from fruit tree to fruit tree on the owner's well-groomed property. A chorus of Ruddy Ground Doves called from their hiding place in a nearby bush. Before long, the sun began to set and several pairs of green parakeets flew by in the distance. Just as a rooster marks the beginning of a new day, these parakeets marked the end with their loud squawking.

As the sun disappeared beneath the trees, things were just about perfect. We were relaxed and happy to have found Playa Uvita, happy to be somewhere new. We had taken a chance, not knowing what we would find down the road less traveled (Roy would be proud), but our risky decision had paid off. We had found our charming hamlet. And with only a few other tourists in sight, it felt as if it was our own little secret.

DAY 8

THE MEANING OF *PURA VIDA*

We turned off the main highway somewhere near San Isidro for San Gerardo de Rivas, a small town at the base of Mount Chirripó, the highest peak in Costa Rica. We were traveling with another couple, Corey and Erin, who was staying a few rooms down at Dagmar. The night before on the shared porch, we noticed them having beers and asked if they wanted to join us. A few too many Imperials later and we had agreed to go with them on a day trip to Cloudbridge Nature Reserve. We were enticed by the promise of a beautiful hanging bridge and misty cloud forest. We also liked the enthusiastic attitude Corey and Erin had about the trip, smiling broadly as they pointed out the route they would take to get there on an oversized fold-out map.

So far, the hour-plus drive had been a joy, similar to the night before. We had a lot in common, all being from Boston, and found it easy to talk for hours. As we passed through Rivas, though, conversation came to a halt. And so did our car. The dirt road abruptly became more like a trail—steep, narrow, and rough—and the bald tires of our compact rental car were having a hard time gripping the loose gravel. As we skidded, the car refusing to advance up the steep pitch, Jenn buried her eyes in her palms. Eventually, we put the car in neutral and slid backwards down the hill. We parked at a local hotel, at the cost of a few dollars, and walked the remaining mile to the reserve entrance.

BUMPY ROADS

To our surprise, several of the roads we traveled on during this trip were nicely paved but don't let that fool you. Much of Costa Rica has bumpy dirt roads with obstacles that can easily swallow an inexperienced rental car driver. On a past trip to the mountains to visit Roy's mom, I was enlisted to drive a small sedan across a rickety bridge made up of just two thick boards. As if Jenn wasn't nervous enough, we then crossed a swift-moving river where the water almost stalled the car's engine. Scenes like this are typical in Costa Rica, so if you do rent a car, make sure it has four-wheel drive and is high off the ground. Otherwise, it's best to stay on the paved roads away from sinkholes, landslides, and washouts.

Studying the maps at Cloudbridge, we soon realized that to get back to Uvita before dark, we needed to speed hike. We knew that driving at night in Costa Rica can be dangerous; in the dark, road hazards that are so common are harder to see and mountain fog can cause poor visibility. Jenn had also read horror stories of hijackings.

With spirits high, we set off up the trail, destined to make it to the hanging bridge and back. At such a high altitude, the landscape was markedly different from the coast. Pine and oak trees grew on the steep, rocky slopes, reminiscent of New England, and thick moss covered much of the foliage. Above, soft gray clouds stalled as they hit the mountains, feeding the greenery with moisture. Below, a series of cascading waterfalls gushed over rocks in a sheet of white, eventually forming a river deep in the valley. Carefully manicured gardens of hydrangeas, impatiens, and lilies created a natural border. Calls and whistles filled the air, but the elusive birds were nowhere to be seen; occasionally a flash of color would almost give them up.

Feeling like goats, we traversed up and down the rocky, mountainous terrain. We followed the well-kept path, descending into the damp valley, until we finally found the bridge. Sun-weathered wooden planks were evenly spaced on the cable system that sagged over a wide stream. Sturdy beams on either side bore our weight as we crossed. The bridge swayed but felt strong. Satisfied to have made it, we traipsed across several times, smiling for the camera, before hustling back to our car.

* * *

Hanging bridge at Cloudbridge Nature Reserve

Happy to be back in the trusty Hyundai, we rode back through Rivas. Not far down the road, we were horrified to see that a car had veered off and was teetering vertically on the edge of a cliff. A tow truck and several locals were already attending to the scene, so we continued on, slowly and carefully.

A few miles down the road, still talking about the terrible accident, we approached a sharp curve. From the opposite direction, a motorcycle came barreling around the corner, over the line. In a split second, we both swerved in a panic. But it was too late. He brushed our back tire, lost control, and crashed violently into the ditch. Erin screamed out from the backseat. Corey, Jenn, and I were speechless—stunned and confused.

Quickly pulling over, the four of us raced down the hill, hoping not to find what we dreaded. As the dust cleared, we saw that the driver was there—alive—standing over his tangled bike. Blood seeped from a shallow cut on the young man's arm as he removed chunks of grass from his scratched helmet. His once immaculate white dress shoes were scuffed, his shirt torn, and skinny dark jeans stained with dirt. He was shook up but alright. I helped him pull his mangled bike from the ditch. Corey, concerned about the cut, found his first-aid kit and tended to the wound. The man didn't speak English, but we could tell that his immediate concern was the damage to the motorcycle and not himself.

We asked if we should call the police, gesturing with our hands. He shook his head no, running his trembling fingers along the bent front forks. Then he looked at our car. There was no damage, just a mark on the tire. As if he suddenly realized how lucky he was to be standing there, alive, he looked me right in the eye and said something I'll never forget.

"*Tranquilo, pura vida.*" (It's okay, everything's tranquil; pure life.)

* * *

Back on the porch in Uvita, still in shock, we reflected. We had left the scene after making sure our surprise acquaintance had a ride. He gratefully shook our hands, thanking us for helping him. Our day would have been so much different if things hadn't turned out the way they did. The man's courage and attitude gave us pause. Yes, his immediate concern was his motorcycle; we could tell from the way he looked at the scuffed paint and broken headlight how much he loved riding that bike. But as if a switch was flipped, his expression changed when we started to leave. More important than his bike, more important than any material item, he was alive, and grateful for our help. To him, everything was "*tranquilo*"; everything was "*pura vida.*" We couldn't agree more.

DAY 9

BICYCLE ADVENTURES AND
SCRUMPTIOUS SNAPPER

The local news blared from our outdated thirteen-inch television. As we sat in bed sipping coffee from mismatched mugs, we did our best to follow as the anchors chattered in Spanish about car accidents, road closures, politics, and other happenings of the day. We were able to understand snippets of what they were saying, commending ourselves when we picked up even a word or two, but it was clear that our Spanish had a long way to go. Sure we could order food in restaurants and get around on the local buses, but beyond the bare basics, we were in the dark. If someone said something to us that wasn't covered in our Spanish workbook, all they got in return was a deer-in-the-headlights look from Jenn and a *no entiendo* from me.

Lucky for us and our lack of Spanish, we didn't have to worry about staying current on the weather. The forecast was a joke: a picture of a sun duplicated seven times and temperatures in the high eighties, signaling more of the same great weather for the next week. We wondered if during the rainy season, they just displayed seven rain clouds.

CLIMATE IN COSTA RICA

Because of its proximity to the equator, Costa Rica enjoys consistently warm temperatures all year long. Some areas are warmer than others, however, depending on altitude. Mountainous regions, such as the Central Valley, are a pleasant seventy to eighty degrees on average throughout the year with cooler temps at night. Coastal locations, at lower altitudes, are generally hotter with temperatures well into the eighties.

Although temperatures remain steady year round, rain is more variable. The timing varies by geographic area, but the dry season is generally from December to April, and the rainy season from May to November (with the rainiest months being September and October). The Northwest Pacific is known to be one of the driest regions. The trees in the Guanacaste province even lose their leaves because water is so scarce during the dry season. Locations farther south, such as the southern Nicoya Peninsula and Central Pacific coast, get more rain and are much more humid. The farther south you go along the Pacific, the hotter and wetter it gets. The Caribbean coast has its own microclimate that brings rain any time of year.

Don't assume that visiting during the rainy season will be a complete washout. Many people actually prefer to visit during the so-called green season because it's less expensive. It typically doesn't rain all day every day, and many activities, like canyoning (rappelling down waterfalls) and white-water rafting, are much more exciting.

After a quick breakfast, we jumped on some bicycles and headed to the highway. It was our last day in Uvita, so we needed to stock up on supplies and withdraw cash from the ATM before leaving for the final leg of the trip. We desperately needed some laundry detergent. All this hot weather had taken a toll on our limited supply of clean clothes, and we still had about five days of traveling to go—too long to just turn things inside out.

The bikes we rented from a place in town were nothing more than a conglomeration of mismatched parts welded together over two wheels, but we couldn't complain for the price. The going rate was two dollars an hour for the first hour and a dollar an hour after that. Getting around by bike was much more fun than walking, or at least so I thought. Jenn was having a tougher time; her bike seat was less than comfortable and each bump emphasized it.

"I don't think there's any padding," she said, jolting the handlebars from side to side to avoid huge rocks protruding out of the dirt.

"Mine's great," I said, joyriding down the road. We tried to switch, but my bike was too tall for her and made the situation even worse.

Almost fell off taking this one; note my intense concentration

After a long, bumpy fifteen minutes, we made it to the highway, each in one piece, and got the supplies we needed. While remounting our bikes, we ran into an older couple living in the area from Falmouth, Maine, close to where we both grew up, small world. It was interesting to talk with these friendly people about what living in Costa Rica was like, especially from the point of view of a New Englander. Costa Rica, it seemed, was treating them well. As they spoke about the great restaurants and beaches they had found in the area, we couldn't help notice how relaxed and happy they were. Even their two adopted dogs seemed to be smiling, their snouts sticking out of the half-opened window of their SUV.

Our destination for lunch was a tiny *soda* we had seen earlier on our trip. It was a place where locals ate: a small, shack-like building tucked beside the dirt road with a long wooden counter and stools made from cut logs. When we walked up, our faces sweaty, a construction worker from a site down the street looked up from his bowl of black beans and rice, giving us the once over. Two women in white aprons eyed us from the kitchen. We were slightly intimidated to sit down at a place like this, but our need for something cold to drink was overwhelming.

Neither of the ladies behind the counter spoke a lick of English, and their Spanish was so fast we couldn't keep up, but somehow we (or I should say, Jenn) managed to order the best meal we had on this trip: perfectly seasoned, whole, pan-seared snapper with fried plantains and a side salad. Jenn had smartly memorized most of the chapter we studied on food—indicative of her priorities—and it certainly paid off in this situation.

Over homemade iced tea, we watched the two women work diligently in the kitchen to prepare these dinner-sized portions. One spooned hot oil over the fish as they sizzled in a pan, while the other used all her weight to press ripe plantains into thin pancakes. Their movements in the kitchen reflected the years of experience they had cooking together. With just a quick glance, one would anticipate the other's next move. The result was a beautiful thing. Thinking that it would be rude to waste even a bite after all that hard work, Jenn and I cleaned our plates and made sure to thank our private chefs before leaving.

Local fare; a slightly larger lunch than we expected

Back at the lodge, we hand washed enough clothes to last through the rest of the trip, and Jenn carefully hung them on the line outside our room, bashfully trying to hide her underwear. Relieved to find shelter from the hot sun, we settled into the recliners on the porch with frosty glasses of beer and did some reading and writing.

While relaxing, we greeted a couple who was taking the room Corey and Erin had just checked out of. We also said hello to José Maria, the owner of Dagmar, who was working in his yard. I asked him about all of his fruit trees, especially curious about the one near our porch that produced melon-sized, spiny green fruit. Within a few minutes, he had retrieved a large chilled slice of this unusual fruit and explained that it was called *guanábana*. The white flesh of the fruit was cool and refreshing as it slid off our forks and surprised our taste buds. Jenn thought it tasted like a mixture of pineapple and coconut, and my very sophisticated and refined palate (self-declared) picked up some citrus notes.

We chatted with José Maria for a while about the many other fruit trees in his yard (banana, lemon, star fruit, and several more with which we were unfamiliar) and were happy to hear that he didn't use any chemicals to grow them. I tried to communicate to him that I was a landscaper and could truly appreciate his hard work, but my words were lost in translation. Instead, I got a quick Spanish lesson on how to correctly say, I am, which I then remembered Soledad also drilling into our heads as, *Yo soy*. Even though we couldn't communicate perfectly with José Maria, Jenn and I could both tell that he was a great guy and took pride in everything he did.

The hours had been moving slower in Uvita. Sure we enjoyed doing something active each day, but we were becoming accustomed to just sitting and relaxing, doing nothing really. I would write in my notebook, while Jenn rummaged through the pages of books trying to identify birds, or we would just stare off at the horizon. We would sip coffee or beer, but at a pace where it would eventually become the temperature of the air, condensation dripping down the glass or bottle. For the rest of the day, we did just that, enjoyed a couple of beers and then some iced coffee, hoping that one would counteract the other.

That night after dinner, we strolled down the main drag. As we ate simple ice-cream cones on a concrete bench, we watched locals go by, some of them on bikes but most on foot. To us, this was the real Costa Rica, the Costa Rica that Roy showed us. We could see how people lived when they weren't working at a tourist shop or luxury hotel. Friendly neighbors sat together on a porch, sharing stories and laughing out loud. A woman swept the front entrance of her well-kept home, while her daughter mended a fishnet in the side yard next door. The sound of children playing and dogs barking permeated the air, accompanied by the thousands of insects singing their evening chorus. To think, we probably would have missed out on all this if we hadn't stubbornly walked down that dusty road that seemed to lead to nowhere. Nowhere turned out to be a magical place.

DAY 10

BREAKFAST BEERS AND
DINNERTIME STORIES

We dashed out of Dagmar, our half-zipped, disheveled bags slung hastily over our shoulders. We were cutting it close but knew that if we walked at a brisk clip, we could probably catch the eight-thirty bus to Palmar Norte. This rushed feeling was just what we were trying to avoid on vacation, but the warmth of sleep had trapped us, luring us to snooze our alarm too many times. With just fifteen minutes to pack and leave, we had chugged our coffee and now it churned in our stomachs.

With the dirt road behind us, we thought we had made it to the highway with plenty of time to spare. But just as we turned the corner, we saw the bus waiting. In a full-on sprint, we made a run for it. Sweat poured off my forehead as the sun beat down. In a sudden burst of adrenalin, I sped by Jenn, leaving her in a trail of dust. As I ran, I could hear snippets of what she was yelling, the rest deafened by passing cars and my heavy breathing.

"Go! Go faster! Hold the bus, you're almost there."

About halfway across the narrow bridge, a giant dump truck came barreling by with an uncovered load of fill.

"Blah . . . yuck," Jenn said, as she tried to wipe the dirt off her face.

When I reached the bus, the doors were closed and the engine was cold. There was no sign of the driver. We had apparently just sweated through our freshly washed shirts and were covered in sludge for no reason. The next leg of our trip was off to a great start so far.

Just after eight thirty, the bus driver came sauntering around the corner, and the small crowd loaded on. The tiny storage area under the bus was already full, so everyone had to climb on with their bags and other belongings. Most of the passengers were Ticos who seemed to be using the bus as their own personal trucking company. Their cargo varied from flat-screen televisions to fifty-pound bags of rice and even crates brimming with water apples, a common fruit from the area. A few tourists took up much of the remaining space with their large bags. One woman, who had been dropped off by a nearby resort, even managed to monopolize a whole row with her five bulging suitcases. I'm fairly sure that this lady didn't need to wash any clothes or hang her underwear out to dry on a porch, she had definitely packed enough.

On the trip south, we traveled through several small coastal towns before the road veered inland through a larger town called Cortés that even had street signs! It appeared that this town had been built up around a new, state-of-the-art hospital. The bus made many stops along the way, and we eyed our watches not knowing how much farther we needed to go. A few of the locals clued us in at each town, letting us know that we still weren't there by holding up their hands in the universal signal for "stop." Sure enough, when we finally did reach Palmar Norte, we had missed the nine-thirty bus. Our connection to Sierpe was long gone.

Stepping off the bus, we were unsure of our next move and even a little taken aback by the fast pace on the streets. Palmar Norte was a bustling town, similar in size to Quepos and with just as much going on around the bus station. After spending the last few days in peaceful Uvita, it was a bit overwhelming to encounter a crowd. Before we had even a moment to worry, in typical Tico fashion, a cab driver immediately came to our "rescue" and offered us his services.

Having seen her concerned Gringa face inside the bus, the cabbie had been trying to get Jenn's attention even before we got off. The astute man, probably making a living off late buses, knew that anyone who had missed the nine-thirty bus would need to take a cab in order to catch the scheduled boat transfer to Drake Bay. Another couple about our age, who had also gotten off the bus, was standing nearby, looking confused. Coincidentally, it was the same couple who had stayed in the adjacent room the night before at Dagmar. Like the taxi driver, we saw opportunity knocking and swooped in to ask if they wanted to split the cab. Hesitant at first, they talked back and forth in French before finally agreeing.

The cab driver whisked us away from the busy town square on a nicely paved road that wound through acres of palm farms and eventually into the small riverside town of Sierpe. To pass the time, Jenn and I chatted with the French couple. The man was pleasant and spoke very good English, but the woman didn't say much and seemed shy. When we were talking about our knowledge of foreign languages, being the proud husband that I am, I, of course, offered up Jenn's skills.

"Jenn speaks some French, you know," I said to the squished trio in the backseat.

With that, the woman excitedly blurted out a string of

sentences in French. Poor Jenn, having no idea what the woman said, had to explain that she had only taken French for a few years in high school and unfortunately didn't remember much. With a disappointed, "Oh," the woman turned back toward her companion and cast her eyes out the window once again.

With Jenn's famous death stare burning into the back of my head, and the language barrier stifling any remaining conversation, our arrival in Sierpe was a much needed breath of fresh air. Sierpe consisted of a menagerie of homes and businesses surrounding one paved road that folded around a tiny square where the town meets the river. Boats on trailers, motorcycles, and trucks were haphazardly parked on either side of the street leading to Centro Turístico Las Vegas, the central station for water taxis to Drake Bay.

We rolled to a stop at the brightly painted cement building that sat perched on the riverbank. As we exited the taxi, a few representatives from lodges in Drake Bay approached, each giving their own unique sales pitch. Once we mentioned our reservations, a representative from our lodge introduced himself and told us that we'd be leaving around eleven thirty.

"I told you they would find us; you know things always work out here," I said, reminding Jenn that she worries too much.

We stepped inside Las Vegas to see other travelers gathered around tables eating breakfast while enjoying the view of the river. Instead of breakfast, we ordered beers, hoping to relax after our hectic morning. The French couple followed suit. As we sat down and started to unwind, we finally learned the names of our new travel companions, Matilda and Julien. It turned out that they hadn't booked a hotel yet, so they began looking through brochures and talking to some of the representatives who were still lurking around.

At the corner of the rough-sawn wooden table, I spent

some time talking to a middle-aged guy from the United States named Mike. He was in the area to check on some property he owned on the Osa Peninsula. Grabbing from a pack of Marlboros in his shirt pocket, he lit a cigarette before sharing his story. Mike, his dirty blond ponytail hanging down his back, told me that the purpose of his trip was to walk and survey the lot with the help of a guide. He went on to explain that the two of them would be hacking through the raw jungle with machetes to mark the parcel's boundaries and make sure no one had been using it. Having always wanted to own property in Costa Rica, I was fascinated to hear about his experience and hung on to every word.

Mike, we found out, was the chatty type, taking long drags from his cigarette and slowly exhaling smoke as he told story after story. Although our conversation was mostly idle chatter, we did learn quite a bit about Drake Bay. Because of poor road conditions and a lack of large docks, goods are shipped to Drake Bay on small boats or four-by-four trucks, making everything very expensive. Having second thoughts about whether we had adequately stocked up on supplies, Jenn went to check out the store. We were not in Uvita anymore; a bottle of mediocre wine was thirty dollars and Banana Boat sunscreen was twenty-eight! Gringo prices for sure. Afraid of what it would be like in Drake Bay when it was this expensive on the mainland, Jenn regretted not buying more in Uvita, but it was too late to do anything about that now.

After our lodge representative found us again, we waited for a few minutes on the narrow wooden dock, sipping water from coconuts while our bags were stowed away. Close by along the riverbank, we watched a large crocodile sun itself while taking a midday nap. I didn't want to tell Jenn, but I could have sworn I saw it open one eye and lick its chops.

On the twenty-foot long, handmade boat, we held onto

life vests alongside fifteen other people. During one of Mike's yarns, he had told us that conditions can get rough at the mouth of the river where the turbulent ocean meets the outgoing current, and that boats have even flipped in the past. I think it would have been better not to know this, especially with crocs in the water, but by this point in the trip, we were beginning to appreciate our more adventurous sides that seldom come out during our daily lives in the States. It was miraculous; Jenn didn't even look nervous, or nauseated.

The trip up the river was amazing. I should preface this by saying that I absolutely love being out on the water. I grew up on a large river in Maine, and although it's harder to get out on the boat now because we live in the city, Jenn and I often get up to Maine in the summer for some fishing (for me) and sunbathing (for Jenn). My bias aside, it seemed as if the other passengers were enjoying the trip too.

Perched up on the boat's benches with necks craned, everyone watched—mesmerized—as we cut through the river's murky brown water, not knowing what lurked beneath. We weaved around floating logs and clumps of plant life. Lush mangroves and tropical rainforest surrounded us on all sides. At one point, we left the main channel and headed straight into the thick of these dense mangroves. At first it seemed as if we were making a landing onshore, but then a narrow channel became visible. The secret passageway was only a few feet wider than the boat and there was no land to be found, just mangroves anchored into the water and the occasional exotic bird passing through.

After steering through the natural maze, we exited into a much larger branch of the river, which widened even more as it led us to the ocean. The millions of gallons of water that had flowed down the Río Sierpe, zigzagging down mountains, through villages and untamed forest, suddenly met its match with the Pacific. The waves coming toward us hit the outgoing current as if they were hitting a beach, cresting and crashing. The turbulent water looked intimidating, but to dodge the worst of it, our boat steered far to the left, though worryingly close to some rocks. Thankfully, our entry into the mighty Pacific was successful, and we were out into the calmer open ocean without incident.

Motoring south along the coastline, we could see a few houses built into the vibrant green hills, but they were few and far between. For the most part, the land was undeveloped and pure. Our boat skipped along the choppy turquoise water at a good pace but soon slowed to a stop when a school of spotted dolphins surfaced. Everyone chirped with excitement and dug out their cameras when the dolphins swam near. I wouldn't be surprised if between all the people on the boat a thousand pictures were taken in the five minutes we were there. As luck would have it, though, most of ours show only the tip of a fin or just open water.

Our best shot of a spotted dolphin

CAMERA RECOMMENDATIONS

Although we are far from professional photographers, we have learned a thing or two about cameras in our travels. If you own a high-end camera, it will most certainly do the trick, but chances are it is also large and heavy. Photo opportunities pop up at the most unexpected times in Costa Rica, so you may want to keep a more compact version with you at all times. Jenn and I have invested in several small digital cameras over the years, upgrading every so often. Our most recent purchase not only has a high megapixel count but is very durable and waterproof down ten feet! We chose this camera over a similar one that offered even more megapixels but had less ability to shoot moving objects.

For video cameras, make sure you have plenty of memory and an extra battery. Nothing is worse than trying to film an amazing adventure and only getting the first half. Whatever camera you choose, keep in mind the types of things you will be photographing or filming. Important ones on our list were landscapes, beaches, sunsets, underwater, and outdoor-action shots of wildlife.

Back underway, it wasn't long before we could see Drake Bay. Houses and *cabinas* were dotted in along the curved shoreline, and small skiffs were moored in the bay. We made a dock landing at a high-end hotel to let a few passengers off, and then double-backed along the shore, making a series of beach landings to unload the rest of us. We waved goodbye to Julien and Matilda at the second stop and wished them luck. At our stop, Jenn and I splashed through the shallow water to the shore in between crashing waves, much like we had for our boat-taxi ride from Montezuma to Jacó. Once safely on the sand, we collected our bags and paid the captain fifteen dollars each for the trip, a bargain for the wonderful tour we'd had.

The walk from the beach to the El Mirador lodge was short but practically straight uphill into the thick jungle; a series of makeshift steps and frayed rope railings made the climb a little easier. The owner, Michael, greeted us at the top, settled us into the open-air dining area, and asked if we wanted some lunch. We felt an air of relaxation emanating from him. Much like Carlos in Montezuma, Michael spoke softly and slowly, taking a moment to contemplate each question before thoughtfully answering.

Before we knew it there were small plates of food and pitchers of freshly squeezed juice and coconut water set out in front of us. Because there are almost no restaurants in town, El Mirador, like most lodges in Drake Bay, included three meals a day in the nightly rate. The welcome we had from Michael and the staff was very warm and would set the pace for the rest of our visit in Drake Bay.

Our *cabina* was halfway down the hill, accessible off the main drive by a short trail through the woods. Set high in the hillside, it had a spectacular view of the bay yet was nestled in the trees enough to give us some privacy. Two of the room's walls consisted of floor-to-ceiling screen windows that brought the outdoors in. Opaque, thin drapes dressed the screens, letting sunlight and a warm breeze filter through and adding to the open, airy feel of the space. Consistent with the back-to-nature theme, the floors were made simply of smooth, unvarnished wooden planks.

* * *

In our bathing suits and flip-flops, we joined Ted on a walk to town. Ted was another guest at the lodge, but he was a lot more than that. A native of Canada, Ted first came to Drake Bay ten years previously. He pitched a tent on the hill at El Mirador and immediately fell in love with the town and its people. Ever since, he has come back for extended visits and is now more like family to the owners than a guest.

We discovered on our walk the tight-knit community that Ted enjoyed so much. As we passed a house, Ted waved to an eight-year-old boy who was placing water apples into a crate for his father to lift into their truck. The boy was a replica of his dad, all the way down to the rubber boots and dirty denim jeans. Later, Ted explained, they would take the fruit to another family in town who would weigh it for shipping. Ted told us that this was the way of life here in Drake Bay, generations growing up and working together to make ends meet.

At one of the only stores in town, we saw another example of community. We watched a clerk offer his own spare batteries to a neighbor because the store was out. This generosity was so intriguing to us; we couldn't imagine something like that happening back in Boston. After spending only a few hours in Drake Bay, we could already appreciate why Ted had fallen in love with this place and kept coming back year after year.

We spent some time exploring the beach and went for a swim afterward to cool off. Ted, happy to keep walking, left us at the lagoon. "Have a good swim, guys," he said. "Just watch out for crocodiles."

"Crocodiles?" Jenn said, her eyes scanning the shallow, crystal-clear water.

"Well yeah, one time me and a bunch of guys were fishing there in that same spot when an eight- or nine-footer started lingering around," Ted said. "But he was just after our bait, I think," he added, smirking, before waving and walking away.

Whether Ted was joking or not, we didn't swim much longer and made sure to keep our eyes peeled for scaly visitors.

* * *

Just as the sun melted into the bay, we sat down for dinner in the dining hall and introduced ourselves to the other guests. Our meal, we learned, would consist of three courses, leaving plenty of time for conversation. Between bites, we talked with an older American couple and a younger couple from Holland who had exciting stories of their journey to Costa Rica through Panama.

The pretty, thirty-something woman with bobbed, curly blond hair recounted being trapped on a bus for ten hours along a Panamanian highway, her warm eyes gazing up over her colorful hipster glasses. Protestors had apparently blocked off the road to draw attention to some questionable new mining laws, even starting several small fires around the bus as it became dark. She had perhaps the sunniest perspective imaginable on what seemed like a terrifying event. Smiling and laughing incessantly, she spoke with such enthusiasm that someone watching from afar would assume that she was talking about the wonderful day she'd had at the spa. Glossing over the fires and angry chanting, she focused on what she and her husband did when the bus finally crossed the border.

"We took out our *Lonely Planet* and found the most expensive resort on the list. We took a cab and checked in, not even thinking about the price; $300, it didn't matter, we deserved it." The couple had been staying mostly at hostels until that night, so the resort was a major splurge.

"We ordered room service, snacked from the minibar, and Gerrit even put on the hotel bathrobe," she continued, finishing the last of her custard dessert. "It was great. And the infinity pool, what a view of the Caribbean!"

Jenn asked, "Would you ever go back to Panama?"

"Well, the bus ride was definitely frightening at times, but I don't think it's something that happens a lot there. And it really could have happened anywhere."

Looking off in the distance, she paused for a moment then began again with a smile.

"There was this little old lady sitting next to me. She must have been ninety, she was so frail. She only spoke Spanish but was trying to reassure me the whole time. She kept grabbing my hand and nodding her head.

"I just remember her staring right into my eyes. She had the most beautiful dark brown eyes; they had this glimmer that brought her wrinkled face to life.

"I don't know what it was, but for some reason, this fragile old woman made me feel safe."

The young woman then looked back at us, the softness gone from her expression.

"But anyway, to answer your question, yes, I would definitely go back to Panama. Everything else about our experience was wonderful, the diving, the people, the food. I wish we could have stayed longer."

Intrigued by these people, Jenn and I ordered some beers for the table and settled in for more stories.

One by one, guests disappeared to their cabins until our group was the last to remain. Following suit, we borrowed a flashlight from the lodge and found our way back to ours.

It had been another long travel day. Usually after maneuvering about on buses and boats we are highly strung and tired, but our first night in Drake Bay was different. We had sprinted to make our bus, missed our connection, and been taken up a river on a boat that could have tipped over at any moment, but we did it with a different attitude. Much like our new friends from Holland, we were learning to take obstacles with a grain of salt, having faith that our difficulties would somehow work out. As our heads hit the pillow, we were feeling quite at peace.

DAY 11

SHRIMP BOATS AND STONE SPHERES

A typical day back home begins with my alarm clock blaring classic rock around quarter past five in the morning. On a good day, I hit the snooze button "maybe once, maybe twice," rallying the energy to get up before it sounds a third time because I feel bad waking Jenn who doesn't have to be up nearly that early. Even with Stevie Nicks singing "Gypsy" in my ear, I find it extremely hard to get motivated when it's still pitch black outside. The winter is even worse. Not only is it still dark when I wake up, but it's a chilling sixty-two degrees outside the covers. Starting the day in our warm, airy cabin cast the exact opposite feeling: Jenn and I were happy to be awake. Not only had we slept great, but we woke to such pleasantries as birds calling, waves crashing, and sunlight streaming in our windows—nature's alarm clock.

We scaled the hill and made it to the dining hall for 6:21 sharp, per Michael's instructions. The night before we had booked a snorkel tour, and Michael told us that breakfast would be served at exactly 6:21 the next morning. Michael had a unique sense of humor. We could tell he enjoyed the confused look on people's faces when they questioned, "6:21? Why not 6:30?" But, nonetheless, Michael was a great person. He was genuinely interested in making our stay enjoyable, asking us if we would rather hang around on the beach and relax or take one of the many tours in the area. Excited to finally be able to do some real snorkeling, Jenn and I jumped at the opportunity to go to Caño Island.

TOURS

In Costa Rica, there seems to be something for everyone. You can zip line through the rainforest canopy, white-water raft along raging rivers, discover the country's more than 880 bird species on a bird-watching tour, or learn how to hang ten at one of the many surfing destinations. Another interesting activity offered in areas with dense rainforest (like Drake Bay) are night tours where, with a headlamp to illuminate your way, you will see poisonous dart frogs, spiders, and other nighttime creatures. Sportfishing tours, whale watching, and sunset cruises are other popular ocean activities, while four-wheeling and rock climbing are available a short drive into the mountains.

To determine if a tour is a good value, calculate what is included (meals, transportation, park fees, equipment?). Also keep in mind that a small portion of what you pay goes to the hotel through which you booked the tour. We were hesitant once to pay seventy-five dollars each for a zip-line tour but pleasantly surprised when we found out that it included door-to-door transportation, an elaborate homemade breakfast, and unlimited drinks.

Caño is a small island ten miles off the coast of Drake Bay. With an intriguing underwater landscape of caves, cliffs, and canyons and extensive reef formations, the waters surrounding the island are known worldwide for diving and snorkeling. But this area doesn't just attract tourists out for a snorkel or dive tour; the rich marine life also draws commercial fishermen out for a quick catch.

On our way out to the island, we witnessed the impacts of shrimp trawling, a method of fishing in which large nets are dragged through the ocean. Scattered around as far as we could see were different species of fish floating belly-side up, the bycatch that had gotten caught in the nets. Our tour guide, Vincent, explained that it was like this every morning, and we could tell that, like us, he was troubled to see the delicate coral reefs and fish destroyed.

After spending a few depressing minutes watching three trawling boats steam along the horizon leaving a trail of dead fish, we finally got going again. No one on our boat would be eating shrimp tonight! We reached the reefs around Caño a few minutes later and were the only boat in sight. Gliding to a stop just off the shore, I peered into the crystal clear water and could already see massive schools of fish. After a few simple instructions from Vincent, one by one we flopped to the edge of the boat in our flippers and jumped into the warm, salty water.

We snorkeled for about an hour and saw many species of brightly colored tropical fish, including enormous schools of jack fish, flashing in a constantly moving sheet of silver. As we swam through these thick blankets of life, the fish wrapped around us, observing us cautiously with their curious eyes. This was what we had been hoping for, clear water and thousands of magnificent fish.

Jenn was maybe a little too excited. While Vincent led the group east along the island, Jenn, her head permanently submerged, paddled her way west. Trying to get her attention, I was the only one who was stuck in the middle. The boat captain, a middle-aged Tico, and his young son were smiling at the situation from the deck.

"Jenn, we're all going this way."

No response, just kicking away in the wrong direction.

"Babe, hey babe!"

Nope, still nothing, she was happy as could be with whatever she was doing.

Finally I caught up to her and she peeled herself away, excited to share that she had been following a sea turtle. The hawksbill, about the size of a Frisbee, glided gracefully through the water, its flippers moving like wings. The amazing animal was about ten feet below her, foraging on the delicacies of the reef. Occasionally, it would rise to the surface, taking a breath, its elongated head and marvelous brown shell only a few feet away. Maybe I should have just trailed off on my own too, I thought, jealous to have missed such a rare creature.

* * *

At the beach near the ranger station, Jenn and I talked with Vincent at some picnic tables while he prepared our lunch. Vincent was a tall, athletic-looking man with short black hair. His florescent yellow water shirt contrasted against his dark skin and hair. As he stood over a ripe pineapple, carefully carving it into bite-size pieces, we quizzed him about the different sea life we had seen and about the island itself. Vincent was a wealth of knowledge, having a detailed and passionate answer for everything we asked.

After learning more from Vincent, we were very curious about the mysterious pre-Columbian stones spheres on top of Caño that are thought to be either ancient burial markers or some type of religious symbol. Intrigued by these ancient artifacts, we decided to break from the group and hike the island for the second part of the tour. To further persuade us to stay onshore, Jenn was feeling slightly queasy from the gallons of seawater now sitting in her stomach.

The trail was steep, slippery, and dark. Based on letters dating back to the late 1500s, historians believe that the explorer Sir Francis Drake landed on Caño, and all I could picture as we walked through the thick jungle were pirates cutting a path with machetes just like in the movies. As we crested the hill, the terrain became flatter. Evenly spaced cow trees let filtered sunlight through, drying the damp ground. We met only a few other people along the trail, but the many birds in the canopy kept us company. As doves cooed from afar, smaller migratory birds seeking refuge from the cold winter zoomed by.

After about forty-five minutes, we came to the end of the trail where two weathered, gray stone spheres sat unassumingly in the brush under a massive tree. The eighteen-inch diameter stones were smaller than what we had pictured, our expectations colored by photographs we had seen of much larger ones in Palmar Norte and Sierpe. Although Caño's spheres were modest in size, their presence ten miles off the coast on top of a small mountain made them intriguing in their own way. We speculated that members of some indigenous tribe must have paddled their hand-carved canoes all the way out to the island and chiseled away for weeks, or maybe even months, to make these perfectly spherical stones.

* * *

Back on the beach, we fought the crowd for a spot to wait for Vincent and the rest of the group. We swam in the crisp, clear water and dried off a bit before they came ashore to retrieve us. Vincent told us that all we had really missed was a small octopus, so we were not regretful of our decision to hike the island. He also told the group that we would spend some time on the way back to Drake Bay looking for dolphins and humpback whales.

The waters between Uvita's whale tail and Caño are a special area for marine mammals. This is one of the only places in the world where humpback whales come to mate and birth young. Mother humpbacks are often spotted milling around these temperate waters with their calves, a tail occasionally slapping the water or mist being sprayed into the air.

Although we didn't see a mystical humpback, there was plenty of other life in the bay. The boat had barely left the shore when a mammoth sailfish sprung from the water. Swimming almost as fast as the boat at full throttle, the spectacular fish flailed itself into the air six or seven times. The acrobatic display highlighted the creature's bright colors, wide dorsal fin, and long, thin bill. For years, I had been trying to catch a fish like that in the Florida Keys on my brother-in-law's boat, always jealous when my dad came back from his vacation showing off photos of him and Albert with gigantic trophies hanging from their lines and even bigger smiles.

With vivid images of sailfish still in our minds, the water once again boiled with activity. This time off the bow a school of spotted dolphins, another frequent visitor to the waters around Caño, appeared. As we circled near, Vincent began banging on the side of the boat and whistling, while signaling the driver to make waves. As if on cue, the dolphins surfaced behind the boat and began surfing in the turbulent water. With the help of Vincent, we had seen a great abundance of marine life in just a short time. But judging by the flurry of activity, it was apparent that we had seen only a small sample of what the bay had to offer. Our splurge on a snorkel tour had proven to be well worth its modest price. We'd had an amazing experience in the water, on the island, and even on the boat ride to and from.

* * *

At sunset we bought a couple of beers and climbed a set of steep steps leading up to the lookout. From one of the highest points in Drake Bay, we had a bird's eye view of the crescent-shaped beach and calm water of the cove. As the sun sank, pairs of green parakeets once again announced the end of the day with their noisy calls. The mating pairs were right on time, flying back to the beach from feeding farther inland, quickly flapping their small wings high in the sky. Finding their roost shortly before sunset after a busy day, it seemed fitting that we were practically doing the same.

Last minutes of daylight in Drake Bay

DAY 12

ATTACKED BY MONKEYS

The one road that runs through Drake Bay abruptly ends when it reaches a muddy lagoon, about the same place where Ted warned us about crocodiles. In the early morning light, Jenn and I ambled over the stagnant water via a long and rickety foot bridge. The head of a well-traveled trail leading to tangled jungle was just around the bend.

Often referred to as a gateway to Corcovado National Park, Drake Bay is the last bit of civilization a hiker will encounter before making it to the San Pedrillo Ranger Station. With no roads along this twelve-mile stretch, accessibility is extremely challenging. The remote beach we were headed to, San Josecito, was just a few miles before San Pedrillo. With such a long hike ahead, we knew that we needed to be careful not to get hurt. Even if we were able to walk back to Drake Bay, Ted had informed us that the area shares a doctor with many other towns, so the likelihood of getting quick medical attention was slim to none. That this didn't bother us in the slightest was a good sign that we had become totally engrossed in the laid-back, *pura vida* attitude of Costa Rica.

CORCOVADO NATIONAL PARK

Corcovado is the largest lowland rainforest remaining on Central America's Pacific coast. One of Costa Rica's biggest national parks, it is noted for vast, untouched wilderness and rich biological diversity. It is accessible only by foot, boat, or small plane, and its remoteness makes it likely that you will be one of only a handful of visitors on a trail at any given time. Everything from Baird's tapir to poisonous dart frogs to jaguars and other big cats live in the park as well as countless species of birds and all four types of monkeys found in Costa Rica.

Corcovado is a park you can explore on your own and many people do. With some planning, you can arrange to stay overnight at the ranger stations and they will even serve you hot meals when you're there. But for many people, visiting with a guide makes the most sense. A popular option, especially for those with limited time, is to take a boat from Drake Bay directly to Sirena Ranger Station, the area of the park that has the most visible wildlife. With the help of a guide's experienced eye, you can see a good sample of what the park has to offer in one day and skip the days of hiking and treacherous river crossings required to reach Sirena.

An occasional incline in the trail's otherwise flat terrain tested our legs and provided great views of the ocean gushing through cavernous rocks in ravines below. The leaf-littered path followed the coastline, weaving on and off of secluded beaches where the only signs of life were some scattered footprints, both human and animal, and shy hermit crabs. Like a picture on a postcard, black craggy rocks flanked the small beaches, providing the perfect resting stop for lazy pelicans, full from an early morning of fishing.

The pristine jungle surrounding us conjured memories of our previous visit to Corcovado National Park. A year earlier, we had gotten a taste of the wonders of Corcovado on a day hike, accessing the park via La Leona Ranger Station on the southern side of the Osa Peninsula. After a grueling two-mile hike from the tiny town of Carate across a shadeless beach, the trail ducked into the jungle's protective canopy. Much like the conditions on our current hike, the weather was extremely hot, creeping into the mid-nineties, even in the shade. The time and effort required just to get to the park entrance made us wonder whether it was worth it, but what we experienced when we finally arrived made the whole trip worthwhile.

Feeling like explorers discovering a new land, we walked along the faint trail through fresh spiderwebs and among strange bird calls high in the canopy. Around every corner, there was something different. Monkeys plucked wild fruit from trees, mother ring-tailed coatis led their babies across the jungle floor, and orange and black Halloween crabs ducked into holes as we approached. All of these animals acted as if they had never seen a human before, and the chances that they had were slim. The vivid memory of that trip was crystalized by the familiar sound of rushing water from the sea, the distinct squawks of Scarlet Macaw parrots, and the humid air rising in dewy droplets off wet sand.

Only able to explore Corcovado for a single day, we have since vowed to return for an extended backpacking adventure. Our rationale for not doing so this time around was that we didn't have the gear to stay overnight or enough vacation time. These explanations were true enough, but the real reason is that we still haven't convinced ourselves that an entire vacation should be spent hiking in extreme temperatures along trails frequented by poisonous insects and snakes; the same trails that also happen to cross shark- and crocodile-filled rivers, passable only when the tide is just right. If the intimidating description in our guidebook wasn't enough, an encounter we had with a German couple exiting the park after a weeklong hike left even more doubt in our minds.

We chatted with the young couple for a few minutes after our hike outside a tiny *soda* in Carate, while sipping cans of natural juices and waiting for the caravan back to Puerto Jiménez. They looked like two people who had just been rescued from a deserted island, their faces tanned and weathered and their clothing dirty and disheveled. When we asked about the hike, they said they had really enjoyed it but couldn't stop saying how hot and tiring it was. They explained that the distance between the ranger stations varied, and that on some days, they had to hike for ten to fifteen hours straight to make it to the next station before dark.

The extent of their fatigue became apparent to us when, while riding on the back of an open-air truck, they fell fast asleep. Jenn and I watched in disbelief as they swayed back and forth, bouncing around on the uncomfortable wooden bench, as the truck traversed over the bumpy dirt road. Laughing at the memory and joking that we would probably feel and look that tired tonight after our one-day hike to San Josecito, we journeyed onward.

As we continued south on the trail, we kept our eyes glued to the trees in search of birds and animals, which are generally more active in the cooler, early morning hours. Sure enough, we came upon a pair of bright red, blue, and yellow Scarlet Macaws eating and squawking boisterously right over our heads in the branches of an almond tree. The crafty birds clung effortlessly to branches with one foot while holding wild almonds with the other, prying at the thick green pods with their arched beaks.

A Scarlet Macaw in its favorite place, an almond tree

When the narrow trail opened into a wide, palm-tree-lined beach, we knew we had made it to San Josecito. With just a few other groups of people, the beach was quiet and tranquil and, thankfully, so was the water. A coral reef and several outcroppings of rock provided a buffer against the ocean's powerful waves and current, keeping the cove's water calm and clear.

Not wanting to waste even a minute of potential snorkel time, we ran across the scalding hot sand and jumped in. Neon blue damselfish, orange and purple Spanish hogfish, and other colorful reef fish zipped around the mounds of gigantic red and brown coral. At one point, Jenn spotted a sharpnose puffer. Excited to share her discovery of the cute yellow creature, she popped her head out of the water to find me.

Before she could, a man who was snorkeling nearby motioned for her to come over. When she approached, the man was standing very still, his dark brown eyes darting left and right, his thick eyebrows raised. Smiling nervously, he lifted his left arm out of the water. Clung to it was a small purple octopus, its smooth skin and tentacles pulsing with color as it felt the fresh air.

"Matt! Matt!" Jenn shouted, splashing the water to get my attention. "There's an octopus over here."

"Huh? A what?" I asked.

"This guy has an octopus," she repeated, pointing to the man's arm and giggling.

When I got closer, I could see that the slimy, eight-legged creature was indeed suctioned to the man's arm. Not knowing quite how to react, I said, "Wow. Thanks." Thinking about it more, I should have said something like, "Are you crazy? That thing is wrapped around your arm, it looks poisonous, and there is no hospital for miles; you must be completely insane!"

* * *

After resting on the beach and having some lunch, we were fully recharged for the journey back to Drake Bay. Happily gallivanting down the trail, we approached another beach where a family of white-faced monkeys was gathered low on the knotty branches of an almond tree. Heavy from the extra weight, the tree's sagging limbs were almost touching the sand. Jenn and I watched the twelve or so of them in awe from about twenty feet away, fascinated by their human-like interactions. While one pair picked insects off each other's skin, carefully smoothing the dark brown fur back into place, another napped, nestled together in a ball. Two of the smallest monkeys jumped from branch to branch in a playful chase that ended in a wrestling match on the beach. Wanting to capture the moment, I got out the camera and knelt down to snap some shots of the cuddly looking creatures.

Just as my knee hit the ground, one of the two-foot-tall monkeys jumped to the sand, stood up on his hind legs, and began barring his long yellow fangs. The mangy, gray white-faced monkey was by far the largest in the group. A scar on his cheek, about the size of my pinky finger, told it all: he was the warrior, the alpha male. Not wanting to cause any trouble, Jenn and I started walking quickly away.

But it was too late.

I glanced back just as two more monkeys leapt from the tree in a fury and joined the angry leader.

All in one second, the three monkeys looked at one another, seeming to confirm their mission, before shrieking and charging us on all fours in a united front. Soon they began to gain on us, and we didn't know what to do. Thinking fast, I remembered Ted saying that this had happened to him before.

"We need to stand up to them. LOOK BIG!"

Jenn immediately stopped walking and turned toward them.

"NOooooooooo!" she shouted in an uneasy tone while pointing her finger at the beasts like a pack of bad dogs.

"Grrrrrrrrr," I added, at the top of my lungs, stomping my feet and raising my arms.

Jenn and I had at least three feet on these fur balls (I towered over them at six feet), but there's something about a wild animal chasing you—no matter the size—that is completely and utterly frightening. As we flailed around, looking like Richard Simmons in a bad '80s aerobics video, the monkeys finally backed down. Glancing at one another, then in our direction with wide eyes, they looked horrified (either that or embarrassed for us). Flabbergasted, we watched Scarface and his posse casually return to their tree as if nothing had happened.

Jenn and I looked at each other and cracked a smile.

"We were just attacked by monkeys!"

DAY 13

A DAY OF BUMPY RIDES

Rays of sun streamed into our *cabina* through small gaps in the canopy above, gently waking us with soft natural light. A warm, salty breeze blew our sheer curtains, making them dance. I looked over at Jenn, and she pouted, pulling up the sheet. We knew that today we were leaving Drake Bay to start our trip home.

The night before, we had stayed at the lookout beyond sunset, trying to absorb every last minute of this magical place. In only the light of a full moon, we watched bats dart through the sky, eating bugs. Below, a small cruise ship was anchored in the bay, defined by a soft glow of orange light. We envisioned its guests relaxing to the beat of a five-piece jazz ensemble, sipping cocktails on the deck. We weren't on a luxury liner but had been more than content sipping from cans of beer to the tune of our own entertainment, waves breaking, frogs croaking, and thousands of cicada chanting loudly in the trees.

When people get back from vacation, they often say that they were ready to come home, their stay had been long enough. As we sat in bed, reflecting on our trip, we decided that these people must be going to the wrong places. Our room didn't have a television, fancy furniture, or even a phone, but it wasn't important, we were happy. Sometimes life becomes overly complicated and the simple parts are forgotten or rushed. Here we felt like we could be entertained for hours just staring out the window.

Shaking the sand from our clothes and packing them away, we eventually faced reality. We did after all have jobs to get back to in just two days. Vacation was coming to an end even if we weren't ready for it. We went up to the lodge for breakfast, thinking maybe food and good company would make us feel better, and it did.

"*Buenos días,*" Gregory said, as he presented our daily fruit plates. "Would you like some eggs, toast, beans, and rice?"

"Yes, please," we both said, smiling from ear to ear.

There we sat for our final breakfast in Drake Bay, sipping coffee and freshly squeezed star-fruit juice. We stayed for a long time, staring out at the vibrant greenery and distant ocean, not wanting to let it go. The dining hall was quiet with only a few other guests; the sound of two blue birds pecking at a hollow tree filled the void.

We ended up talking to Gregory for a while, the same familiar face we had seen for three meals a day for the last three days. With fewer tables to tend to, we finally learned more about our new friend and got to hear his perspective on living in a place we considered paradise. Not surprisingly, he greatly appreciated the natural world around him.

* * *

After collecting our bags, we walked down to the beach one last time. At the foot of the hill on the edge of the sea was a mural that had been painted by the staff at El Mirador. The colorful scene depicted the lodge, complete with dining hall, local wildlife, and even the family cat and dog. Painted to the left was a quotation; what it said made our eyes well up.

> What's more important?
> To know where we came from
> And where we're going
> Or to live in the present?

Often in life, we don't fully appreciate things until they are taken away. Everyone knows that we must make the best of every minute, but this message is often forgotten. The stress of work and everyday responsibilities—that seem so important in the moment—somehow take over and life's simple joys are lost. It happens to us all.

Since having suddenly lost people we held dear, Jenn and I know all too well that life can be cut short at any moment. Because of this, we have endeavored to change our priorities. We now strive to maintain perspective in our daily lives on what's important and appreciate even the smallest, seemingly insignificant moments. It is for this reason that we return to Costa Rica year after year. The unhurried pace of life, simple culture, and beautiful environment slow us down and remind us to appreciate every moment we have—to live in the present.

We sat on a sun-bleached, silver log and gazed out at the bay, watching the boats and local fishermen in their daily routines. It was humbling to know that even after we left, life would continue on here just as it was today. We snapped some photos and did our part by picking up a few pieces of trash scattered about the otherwise pristine beach. Much too soon, it was time to meet Michael, who would be our taxi to the Drake airstrip.

* * *

As we waited at the bottom of the driveway, Michael rushed by on his four-wheeler, shouting over his shoulder that he was going over the ridge to his parent's house to get the four-by-four Isuzu. Even at a slow crawl, the durable SUV proved to be no match for the bumpy dirt road, which Michael informed us can be flooded and impassable during the rainy season. On the way, we passed several small houses and farm fields, even crossing one of the rickety wooden bridges that are so common throughout Costa Rica.

Not far up the road, we stopped to snap a few pictures of some more pre-Columbian stone spheres, sitting prominently in someone's yard. At about three-to-four feet in diameter, they were much larger than the ones on Caño Island and just as mysterious. That someone, hundreds of years ago, chose to place those spheres in Drake Bay said a lot about the sacredness of this remote village.

Pre-Columbian yard ornaments

The Drake "airport" looked more like a bus stop than an airport with a corrugated aluminum roof covering a sitting area that was open on three sides. The bathroom was also quite exposed, consisting of a toilet surrounded by a three-foot high cement-block wall on one side and a cow pasture on the other. I don't think the building had electricity, which was good for us because there was no scale to weigh our likely over-the-limit bags. In typical Tico style, there were, however, several airline employees well dressed in uniforms to check us in and make the experience as professional as possible.

Looking to the sky, there was no sign of our plane. Jenn and I would have been fine if it didn't come, but eventually we heard the buzz of the engine over the trees. As the twenty seater touched down, a tourist from Canada informed us that the Twin Otter was the best bush plane available (and made in Canada, of course). The plane was running late but swung around at the end of the tarmac, unloaded the arriving passengers, and was ready for us all too soon. We waved goodbye to Michael, who was helping the airline workers stow away our luggage, one last time through the small porthole windows.

The Drake airstrip

From high above as we headed north, we could see the Río Sierpe and then the marine reserve in Uvita, marked by the whale-tail-shaped point. Right before we started to head inland, Manuel Antonio and Quepos also came into view. Closer to the mountains, it became a lot cloudier and the turbulence kicked up. The small plane bounced up and down and from side to side, but the trusty pilots calmly adjusted some instruments to smoothen the ride.

The landing at Tobías Bolaños, San José's airport for charter planes, was a different story. As we neared the capital city, strong winds jolted the plane in all directions. From our seats just behind the pilots, we had a clear view of the approach to the runway. In silence, Jenn and I watched the stationary black airstrip move in and out of view as we erratically swayed through the air. Other passengers leaned back in their chairs with their eyes closed as we made our descent. We were jolted once more, then flattened out at the last minute and made a perfect landing. Relieved to be on solid ground, Jenn turned around and looked at me, her face a clammy eggshell white. The look I got when she realized that I had been happily filming video the entire time was priceless.

In complete contrast to the busy international airport, we stepped out of the double doors of Tobías to just a few taxi drivers leaning against a wall. We waited beside them for the bus to San José. When it arrived, the driver asked in Spanish if we were transferring to Alajuela (or so we thought), and I confirmed. It seemed he would tell us where to get off, so we felt fairly comfortable we were on the right bus.

We traveled through suburban neighborhoods for a long time before passing the new soccer stadium and heading into San José proper. Still with no signal from the driver, we started to get nervous when we noticed several other buses bound for Alajuela traveling in the opposite direction. The Tico in front of us, a young guy who was about eighteen, must have been eavesdropping because he asked where we were going. I told him Alajuela, and he signaled for us to wait, using the same international sign that the locals gave us on the bus to Palmar Norte. At the next stop, near the Coca-Cola bus terminal, he told us to get off with him.

We followed obediently all around San José, crossing several streets and trying not to lose sight of him in the droves of people. In the back of my mind, I hoped we weren't being lured into a trap as the three of us weaved through the mixture of street vendors, homeless people, ladies of the night, students, and working class Ticos. About ten minutes went by, and much to our relief, our volunteer tour guide stopped and pointed at a waiting bus clearly labeled Alajuela.

I asked our new friend if he was taking that bus too, hoping to pay his fare, but he pointed back in the other direction. I tried to offer him money, but he refused. He just shook our hands and smiled, keeping his head low as if he was embarrassed. We thanked him repeatedly before jumping onto the idling bus. Even in the hustle and bustle of the city, the kindness of the Costa Rican people still shined.

We got our bearings in Alajuela and walked the few blocks to Los Volcanes, the hotel at which we had hoped to stay on our first night in Costa Rica. This time they had some vacancies, and we settled into a contemporary and inviting room. With neatly folded linens, polished tile floors, and a window that actually closed, it was nothing like the miserable hostel we'd stayed at before. Although we knew we would sleep better here, by this point in our trip, we were much more relaxed and probably would have been fine at the hostel. We might have even joined in on a late night game of bridge.

On our first day in Costa Rica, we didn't explore Alajuela because we arrived so late and were intimidated by the unfamiliar surroundings. Today we had time and felt a lot more comfortable, so we decided to see what the city had to offer. After dropping off our bags, we walked toward the central square. A bustling indoor market on the way drew us in.

Vendors hawking everything from fish to cheese to household items were shouting prices and daily specials. Tica women with their kids in tow selected provisions for that night's dinner, choosing from the array of meat and colorful farm-fresh fruits and vegetables. A man selling lottery tickets counted a stack of coins, while teenagers in baseball hats grabbed Coca-Colas from a cooler. An old man cobbling a belt on a wooden stool glanced up at us and smiled.

When we first arrived in Costa Rica, we felt out of place. We held our guidebook low and were embarrassed by our pale skin and lack of Spanish. Today, as we weaved through the daily lives of these Ticos, we felt surprisingly comfortable. Not because we were tanned and didn't have our gigantic backpacks, but because we shared something with these people. We understood what Costa Rica was about. The laid-back demeanor, the appreciation for the simple parts of life—we felt it. We had experienced it, at the rodeo, in the small towns we had visited, and even on the bus. We had become more like them, more *pura vida*, even in two short weeks.

DAY 14

BRINGING *PURA VIDA* HOME

In the dim morning light, we rode the shuttle to the dreaded airport. The trip took only about ten minutes but seemed to last far longer. The other Gringos in the van were already talking about their jobs and the frigid winter weather back home, a reality we were not at all ready for. To make matters worse, with early morning temperatures in only the mid-sixties, we had traded in our shorts and flip-flops for pants and sneakers. Yes, we were still in Costa Rica, still on vacation, but the city-like feel of Alajuela made it apparent that we were one step closer to home. After all, where were the soothing waves that lapped the shores of Uvita, and the smell of a warm, salty breeze we already missed from Drake Bay? Where were the bird calls that woke us up in Manuel Antonio, and the cool mist that enveloped us in Chirripó's cloud forest? As we stared silently out the window at the blocks of dull concrete, I wondered, were we finally raising the white flag, admitting that our vacation was over and calling it quits?

Looking at one another, rolling our eyes, we both knew we wouldn't give up that easy. We had already discussed that the plan as usual was to have fun on the way home, squeezing every last minute out of the time we had. We would find the best place to eat and have the tallest beers available during our layover. We would make every effort to keep our *pura vida* mentality and try to live in the moment. The San José airport, we knew, would be a major test.

The airport greeted us with long, unorganized lines, which wrapped around flimsy people barriers and seemed to lead to no particular airline kiosk. We managed to find other travelers on our flight and waited alongside them for the ticket counter to open. If Costa Rica was trying to tell us something, maybe it was that we should forgo this painstaking process and just stay. Unfortunately, it was too late for that.

NAVIGATING THE AIRPORT

During peak travel months (December through March), San José's international airport is swamped with confused tourists, all trying to figure out where to go and what to do. The process is actually fairly straightforward once you've gone through it.

The first step is to pay your departure tax (twenty-eight dollars at the time of this writing) to the Costa Rican government at the far right side of the airport. You can pay the fee in US dollars, colones, or by credit card and will need to present your passport. If you pay with credit, the transaction will be processed as a cash advance.

After you've paid the tax, you will be given a form to fill out, which allows you to check-in for your flight. The line to check-in may be long. Not only that, but the airlines often don't have anyone

---

working at the desk until much closer to the time of departure, so you don't know where to stand. With this recipe for disaster, the best way to make sure you don't miss your flight is to arrive the full recommended time before departure, ask an airport official which line to get in, and watch the monitors.

After hours of waiting, we finally reached the ticket kiosk. The friendly Tica behind the counter was polite and welcoming as she produced our boarding passes; the mass of cranky, sunburned tourists didn't seem to faze her in the slightest. At the security checkpoint, our crippling addiction for coffee was somehow undetected, allowing us to pass through quickly. Before finding our gate, we made a beeline to the food court to purchase two cups of the black magic. We thought we were being smart by buying our coffee before getting on the plane but enjoyed only a few sips before realizing that we were about to go through another security check.

We had forgotten that in Costa Rica they do an additional baggage search while boarding the plane. Not only did they confiscate our coffee, but they also took our Chilero. We had tried this delectable hot sauce on our eggs one morning in Uvita and really wanted to bring some back; not just because we liked the taste, but because it reminded us of that wonderful breakfast on the porch at Dagmar. Like a true lawyer, Jenn zealously pleaded her case to the airport officials, trying to convince them to bend the liquids' rule and let the just over three-ounce container on the plane. She employed Spanish whenever possible and even gave the young Tico her best Bambi eyes (blink, blink), but nothing seemed to work. Sadly, the Chilero was added to the pile of confiscated items. After guzzling what we could of our piping hot coffee, we boarded the plane.

I plopped down in the window seat and stared out beyond the chain-link fence bordering the runway. Jenn leaned over me and peered out too, hoping to catch one more glimpse of paradise. The looming green mountains were dotted with red, orange, and gray roofs, and terracotta-colored dirt roads trailed off, connecting to small towns and farms. We thought about the people who lived in those modest homes. They may not have a lot but for the most part they're happy—living life and appreciating the small things that each day brings. We may have lost our coffee and hot sauce, but these material things weren't important; we were still bringing Costa Rica home with us. Whenever we wanted and wherever we were, we could close our eyes and go back.

Costa Rica, its gracious people and magnificent beauty, will imbed itself in your soul, change you for the better, and leave you wanting more. It is more than a vacation destination but only if you want it to be. Take time to meet the people, see how they live, and compare them to yourself. Get out of your comfort zone and try something new; live a little, you won't regret it. You won't fully understand until you visit for yourself, but once you do, Costa Rica will become a part of you. Someday, you may find yourself tangled in the stress of life and whisper,

"Pura vida."

* * *

To follow our next adventure, get more travel advice, and see photos and videos, visit us at http://www.twoweeksincostarica.com.

Find us on Facebook at http://www.facebook.com/TwoWeeksInCostaRica.

Follow us on Twitter at @2wksinCR.

APPENDIX A:
PACKING

Packing has changed greatly for us over the years. When we first started traveling far from home, we each brought large suitcases and carry-ons, making sure we would have everything we'd ever need and more. Our outlook quickly changed when, on our first trip to Costa Rica, our luggage never made it onto our connecting flight and didn't catch up with us until the fourth day of our one-week vacation. If it wasn't for Roy communicating with the airline for us in Spanish, I'm not sure we would have ever seen our bags again.

We have since learned many lessons on what we actually need to bring and now travel with only carry-ons. Packing a two-week vacation into a tiny bag can be a daunting task and requires plenty of planning. Luckily, Costa Rica is a very casual country, so you can probably leave at least five of those seven pairs of shoes at home. Although this method is not for everyone, you should think hard about which items you really need for your trip and which can be left to chance (or purchased once you arrive).

In addition to the obligatory flip-flops and sunglasses, you'll of course need plenty of clothes. Consider where in Costa Rica you'll be visiting, the climate there and what activities you want to do. For instance, if you plan to hike, be sure to bring appropriate footwear (hiking boots or sturdy sneakers) and lightweight articles that dry quickly (look for fabrics that wick away moisture).

In most areas of Costa Rica, you'll need only shorts and tee-shirts year-round, as temperatures remain steady in the seventies or eighties. There are, however, some exceptions to this general rule. For example, higher altitude locations such as Chirripó National Park, the Monteverde Cloud Forest, and many of the volcanoes can be on the cooler side (averaging sixty to seventy degrees and sometimes cooler at night), so you will want to pack pants, long sleeve shirts for

layering, and a light jacket. If you plan to visit during the
rainy season (generally May to November), you'll want
waterproof footwear and a rain jacket or poncho.

As with any trip, you'll need to use common sense in
determining what to bring. We won't go into excruciating
detail here and instead provide below a list of miscellaneous
items that you might not think of:

- Voltage adapter. Costa Rica's standard voltage is
  120 V, the same as in North America. Consider
  whether you'll need an adapter for your cell-phone
  charger, laptop, or other electronic device.
- Binoculars
- Poncho
- First-aid kit
- Compass
- Small container of laundry detergent
- Small backpack for day hikes
- Alarm clock or watch with an alarm
- Map of Costa Rica (especially if you will be renting
  a car)
- Insect repellent
- Flashlight or headlamp (a must if staying in a
  remote area)
- Spanish dictionary

APPENDIX B:
BANKING AND CURRENCY

We've been in the unfortunate situation of getting to Costa Rica and realizing that our bank had not properly authorized our cards for international use. Without being able to access our cash, we had to take out a cash advance on our credit card to pay our bill at a hotel. It worked but was stressful and a bit of a pain to have to wait in line (for hours) at the bank when we could have been out enjoying the day.

To make sure this doesn't happen to you, call your financial institutions before you leave. Note that some banks, like Bank of America, require you to authorize your credit cards and debit cards separately, even if all your accounts are through the same bank.

Most businesses in Costa Rica will take credit, so you don't have to carry a lot of cash. If you do run out, there is typically an ATM in most towns. ATMs will dispense both colones and US dollars. Both forms of currency are accepted everywhere in Costa Rica, but it's best to carry some local currency for bus and taxi fares to avoid overpaying. If you pay in US dollars, the driver will need to calculate the conversion and will probably err on the side of undercompensating you. It's always a good idea to do some quick math in your head before handing over bills that will require change, although we have never run into a situation where we have been shorted.

Once you've authorized the cards you want to bring, remove any unnecessary ones from your wallet. That way if your wallet is lost or stolen, you won't lose everything. It's also a good idea to write down the account and credit card numbers you plan to use as well as the international customer service number of your financial institution, and store them away in a safe place other than your wallet. This ensures that you will be able to contact your financial institution and access your accounts in case of emergency.

APPENDIX C:
BOOKING A HOTEL

If you haven't booked accommodations in advance, you have the advantage of checking out a hotel before committing to stay. Hotels are happy to show you a room and usually have someone on the premises who can speak at least some English and is able to answer basic questions. In more rural areas, it is less common to find English speakers, so you may have to brush up on your Spanish. [See the simple checklist below for some key Spanish words.]

Accommodations vary from simple hostels to cozy bed and breakfasts to extravagant resorts with all the bells and whistles. Open-air *cabinas*, like the one we stayed at in Drake Bay, are common in coastal towns. Prices range from ten dollars a night for a shared room at a hostel to $300 plus a night at high-end hotels and resorts. You can find a decent midrange hotel with a private room, hot water, and air conditioning for forty to sixty dollars a night. When considering hotels, keep in mind that room rates are often negotiable, especially if you're staying more than one night or during the low (rainy) season. Another potential way to save money is to pay in cash; hotels often give a discount for not using credit.

Finally, we would be remiss if we didn't mention some important differences in the Costa Rican bathroom. Probably the most shocking to foreigners is that many hotels, even nicer ones, will ask that you do not flush toilet paper down the drain and instead place it in the wastebasket. The reason for this is that sewer and plumbing systems in most towns are extremely simple and paper products can overwhelm them very quickly.

The second major difference is that some hotels (mostly low-budget options) do not have hot water for showering. In many areas of Costa Rica where it is extremely hot, this is not a problem, but hot water is nice to have in the mountainous cooler regions. Mid-range and luxury hotels usually do have hot water, but don't expect your shower experience to be the same as back home. In all but the most luxe hotels, hot water is provided via a "suicide shower," so named because an electric heater is attached to the showerhead, often complete with exposed wires. Combining water and electricity may seem downright scary; however, these showers have been used for years throughout Latin America and are safe when used properly.

Hotel checklist:

- Private or shared bathroom? (*¿Baño privado o compartido?*)
- Hot water? (*¿Agua caliente?*)
- Air conditioning or fan? (*¿Aire acondicionado o ventilador?*) Is it working?
- Refrigerator? (*¿Refrigerador?*)
- Kitchen? (*¿Cocina?*) If you plan on cooking, make sure the kitchen has everything you need (pots and pans, plates, utensils).
- Internet access? (*¿Acceso a Internet?*)
- Does the hotel accept credit cards? (*¿Acepta tarjetas de crédito?*)

APPENDIX D:
TRANSPORTATION

Bus

Although public buses can be intimidating, they're a great, inexpensive option and can get you to and from almost anywhere in the country. There are two types of buses in Costa Rica: *colectivos* and *directos*. Most buses are *colectivos*, or local buses that make frequent stops. *Directos* generally serve farther destinations and stop much less frequently. In general, you don't need to buy tickets (*tiquetes*) in advance for local buses and can pay your fare directly to the driver. But for longer trips (for example, to and from San José), it's a good idea to buy your tickets in advance because they may sell out.

If you opt to travel by bus, arrive at the bus stop early and ask about departure times (the day before if possible). Buses are not always running on schedule, and the times provided in guidebooks can be outdated. In addition, because *directos* typically run less often than *colectivos*, it is especially important to arrive early because the next direct bus may not be for several hours or even the next day.

Here are some more tips for making your bus trip a success:

- Although there are usually signs in the front window with the point of origination and destination, they are not always accurate so it's a good idea to speak your destination to the driver when you get on. You'll probably need to hone in on your Spanish skills, as we found that the drivers usually don't speak English, but they do understand some.

- Sit near the front and keep an eye out. If your guidebook has a map of the area, use it to orient yourself by looking for signs and landmarks, such as parks, soccer fields, and churches.

- Look for other Gringos on the bus and don't be

afraid to ask them if you're unsure about where to get off; they may know more than you and be able to help.

- Figure out which side will get the most sun and sit on the other one. Most buses don't have air conditioning, so sitting in the sun in eighty-plus-degree heat can get uncomfortable, especially if you're stuck in traffic. You'll notice that the Ticos are keen to this.

Shuttle Bus

An alternative to the public bus is a tourist van/shuttle bus. Interbus and Gray Line Costa Rica are two companies that offer this service. They provide door-to-door service, picking you up at your hotel and dropping you off at your next destination. For this convenience, you'll pay much more than you would for the public bus (from thirty-five to ninety dollars per person). But for some travelers, the extra cost is worth the comfort of air conditioning and more leg room. You may want to book your tickets in advance, as these vans hold only eight to nineteen passengers and fill up fast.

Taxi Cab

Taxis are common across Costa Rica and very affordable. Most are red or maroon with a yellow triangular symbol on the door, a beacon on the roof, and a meter on the dash. Official airport taxis are orange with the same markings but may cost you a little more. You may also find "pirates," so named because they steal business from the regulated drivers. These folks use similar looking cars but don't have a meter or the proper licenses. Ride with pirates at your own risk and always ask for a quote before you do; even the pirates know the going rate.

Small Plane

For a reasonable price if booked in advance, puddle-jumper planes can save time when traveling long distances within Costa Rica. Two companies that offer flights are Nature Air and Sansa Regional. Not only will taking a plane help you avoid often painstaking travel along slow, bumpy roads, but the view from a couple thousand feet up is outstanding. And unlike on commercial airlines, you can keep your camera handy for some great aerial shots. Planes range from five to twenty seaters and can get a little bumpy when traveling through the clouds. Think of it as an amusement park ride with a view!

Water Taxi

Water taxis can also save you time when traveling from one coastal (or lakeside) destination to the next. Look for them to get from Arenal to Monteverde on Lake Arenal, from Sierpe to Drake Bay, from Cariari or Moín to Tortuguero National Park, from Puntarenas to Paquera, from Montezuma to Jacó, etc. These taxis vary from ferries to speedboats to rowboats, so make sure you ask before buying your ticket.

Renting a Car

If you're brave enough to drive Costa Rica's wild roads and want the independence of having your own car, there are plenty of rental agencies near airports and in popular tourist towns. When selecting a vehicle, go with something higher off the ground and with four-wheel drive, if possible, like an SUV. Roads in Costa Rica can turn from smooth pavement to rocky dirt in a flash, and you don't want to lose a tire in the middle of nowhere. On that topic, get the added full-coverage insurance. Even if you would normally opt out of this back home, it will give you peace of mind in case something does happen.

The most important advice is to never leave any belongings inside the car. Thieves can tell which cars are rentals, and as our rental agent told us, picked locks are the most common full coverage claim. More serious crimes are likely to occur at night, so it's best to avoid driving after dark. Also, be sure to park your car somewhere safe like a business or guarded lot instead of just leaving it unattended on the side of the road or beach.

APPENDIX E:
DINING

The prices in restaurants are higher than in most other Latin American countries but still very reasonable. One person can eat for about twenty dollars a day, so long as they are willing to eat lots of rice and beans. Those on a more moderate budget can get a great three-course meal including drinks for less than thirty dollars per person. In general, areas that cater to tourists are pricier than lesser-known towns that the guidebooks have not yet discovered. On a recent trip to the Osa Peninsula, Jenn and I found a restaurant on the outskirts of Puerto Jiménez that served us *casados* (plates of fish or meat and a small salad, vegetables, and beans and rice) for less than six dollars each.

Something else we've learned is that you need to ask for the bill. On our first trip, we were perplexed as to why servers didn't bring the check after we'd finished our meals and told them, sometimes several times, that we didn't want anything else. Eventually we figured out that Ticos, being the very polite people that they are, will wait until you request the bill so that they don't seem rude. The magic Spanish words are, "*La cuenta, por favor (la-kwen-ta por fa-vor)*." When you get the bill, it may be in colones, US dollars, or both; it depends on the restaurant. Ten percent gratuity for service (*servicio*) is usually included and the servers don't expect more, but we like to give a little extra for exemplary service. Finally, if you don't see something on the menu, it doesn't mean they don't have it. Most restaurants (even cafés) have beer, wine, and bottled water, so it doesn't hurt to ask.

ACKNOWLEDGMENTS

Writing *Two Weeks in Costa Rica* was a new and exciting challenge for us. We owe sincere gratitude to our friends and family for their love, guidance, and support throughout the long, and sometimes arduous, writing process. Special thanks to Ronnie French, Mathias Rosenfeld, Erin Schenck, Corey Schenck, Lindsey Spagnola, and Courtney Queen for their invaluable input and editorial assistance. Your feedback really helped us focus the draft. Thanks are also in order to Erin Schenck for her insightful marketing assistance. We also got technical assistance and crucial help with cover design from Cara Mottola and Matthew Nelson. Finally, special thanks to Gary Smailes from BubbleCow for his thoughtful edits and suggestions, which really helped give the book depth and clarity. We thank all of you so very much.

Also, *muchas gracias* are owed to our dear Tico friend Roy Alexander Azofeifa for introducing us to the wonders of Costa Rica. Without him, this book wouldn't exist.

SUGGESTED READING

Firestone, Matthew D., Carolina A. Miranda, and César G. Soriano. *Lonely Planet: Costa Rica*. 9th ed. Footscray, Victoria, Australia: Lonely Planet, 2010.

Forsyth, Adrian and Ken Miyata. *Tropical Nature: Life and Death in the Rainforests of Central and South America*. Clearwater, FL: Touchstone Books, 1984.

Howells, John. *Choose Costa Rica for Retirement: Retirement, Travel, and Business Opportunities for a New Beginning*. 9th ed. Guilford, CT: Globe Pequot Press, 2009.

Kohnstamm, Thomas. *Costa Rican Spanish*. 2nd ed. Footscray, Victoria, Australia: Lonely Planet Publications, 2011.

Lawson, Barrett. *A Bird-Finding Guide to Costa Rica*. Ithaca, NY: Cornell University Press, 2009.

Reid, Fiona A., Twan Leenders, Jim Zook, and Robert Dean. *The Wildlife of Costa Rica: A Field Guide*. Ithaca, NY: Cornell University Press, 2010.

Van Rheenen, Erin. *Moon: Living Abroad in Costa Rica*. Edited by Sabrina Young. 2nd ed. Berkeley, CA: Avalon Travel, 2007.

Wagner, Henry R. *Sir Francis Drake's Voyage Around the World: Its Aims and Achievements*. San Francisco, CA: J.J. Gillick & Co., 1926.